T0153589

INCULTURATION

Working Papers on Living Faith and Cultures

edited by

ARIJ A. ROEST CROLLIUS, S.J.

XIV

CENTRE "CULTURES AND RELIGIONS" - PONTIFICAL GREGORIAN UNIVERSITY

Valeer Neckebrouck

RESISTANT PEOPLES
THE CASE OF THE PASTORAL MAASAI
OF EAST AFRICA

ROME 1993

ISBN 88-7652-663-3

Editrice Pontificia Università Gregoriana
Piazza della Pilotta, 35 - 00187 Roma

TABLE OF CONTENTS

Introduction	1
Missiology	5
Nomadism	9
An Unfortunate Experience	11
Prosperity	13
Isolation	17
The Military Ordeal	21
An Innate Mentality	23
Unadapted Acculturation	27
The Ecological Argument	29
The Dynamics of Social Relations	35
Ethics	49
Socialization	65
Final Determinations	73
Bibliography	77

About the Author

Valeer Neckebrouck, born in 1936, Korbeek-Dijle (Belgium), is a priest of the archdiocese of Malines-Brussels. He is doctor in theology and doctor in anthropology. After having worked for then years as a Fidei Donum priest in Rwanda and Zaïre, he spent five years as an anthropologist among the agricultural Kikuyu and the pastoral Maasai of Kenya. He also did anthropological field-work in Ethiopia, Peru and Honduras, and made extensive study tours to several other African and Latin American countries. Since 1982 he combines these activities in the field with teaching, first at the Faculty of Theology of Tilburg (the Netherlands), later at the Faculty of Theology and at the Centre for Social and Cultural Anthropology of the Catholic University of Louvain (Belgium). He is the author of several books and numerous articles on anthropology, missiology and theology.

INTRODUCTION

Within the course of two millennia, Christianity has succeeded in one way or another and albeit to different degrees respective of the regions, in implanting itself in the majority of the countries of the world. Regarding itself as a religion with a universal vocation, this result corresponds to the expectations of its members and propagators. That which poses a problem for them is rather the fact that this universal destiny has not been realized in a more convincing way. In Asia Christianity is represented by only a minute minority. In other non-Western countries, its presence is limited to a handful of European or American expatriates. And even in countries where Christian preaching has met with an undeniable success, certain ethnic groups refuse collectively and with obstinacy, to join the Christian ranks. This state of affairs raises among other problems, the question of the relationship between a particular religious ideology, here Christianity, and socio-economic formations which may or may not be capable of integrating it, which may or may not be disposed to assimilate it. In other words, I am referring to the phenomenon of the resistant peoples.

Kenya and Tanzania are two bordering countries where Christianity has been in general well received almost from the outset. Still today, it is in full flight. How come that, within the context of general benevolence toward the new religion, the Christian missions have not been able to take foothold among the different sections of the Maasai people who live there? Ancient sources and contemporary studies are in agreement in attesting that, surrounded by Bantu people who have all responded positively to the missionary action, the Nilotic Maasai[1] have never ceased opposing with a categorical no the call of the missions, and this in spite of a long presence of the latter among them. In the beginning, nevertheless, someone as Mgr. Le Roy did not lack optimism. A century ago he wrote:

---

[1] Without being complete, the most elaborate bibliography on the Maasai to date can be found in F. Mol, *Maa. A Dictionary of the Maasai Language and Folklore* (Nairobi: 1978) 177-190.

1

Sera-t-il possible un jour – on voudrait dire bientôt – de bâtir sur ce fond étrange l'édifice religieux dont Dieu nous a révélé l'ensemble? de rétablir les points oubliés ou déformés? de compléter les lacunes existantes? de baptiser ce peuple extraordi-naire, que peu d'Européens encore ont étudié, ou nulle mission ne s'est établie? Pourquoi non? Il y faudra sans doute mettre beaucoup d'énergie, de patience, de tact, de prudence, beaucoup de sueurs, peut-être un peu de sang. Il faudra vivre de sa vie nomade, se faire à ses habitudes étranges. Mais rien de tout cela n'est au-dessus de la puissance d'un missionnaire qui tient son mandat de l'Eglise catholique et que soutient la grâce de Dieu.[2]

But forty years later, another missionary noted that, taking into consideration the number of years that the mission had been active amongst the people, the results proved to be extremely disappointing. He specified that, in spite of the persistent and enduring efforts of the missionaries, in 1936 there were less than two hundred Christians among the Maasai of Kenya, whose numerical power was then estimated to be close to fifty thousand.[3] Research conducted in 1981-1982 within the same population, which at that time counted 231,290 persons, identified among them eleven thousand Christians.[4] The survey reveals to which point the diagnoses of D. Barrett, who in the same year evaluated the proportion of converted Maasai to be of twenty percent, were exaggeratedly optimistic.[5] We would venture to say that even the more modest number based on the survey should at present be interpreted in a more restrictive sense. However small this number is, I have good reason to suspect that it includes a certain number of immigrants, mainly Kikuyu, who often have not been distinguished from the Maasai,[6] not in the least because they themselves conceal their true ethnic origins

---

[2] A. Le Roy, *Au Kilima-Ndjaro* (Bruxelles, 1894) 432-433.

[3] A. Philip, *New Day in Kenya* (London - New York, 1936) 57. P. Julien, *Zonen van Cham. Onder Oost-Afrikaanse Steppevolken* (Amsterdam, 1958) 238, speaks of one hundred and fifty Catholics for the whole tribe in 1958.

[4] K. Shingledecker, *Unreached Peoples of Kenya. A Summary Report of Research* (Nairobi, 1984) 33. For details on the geographical distribution of Christian Maasai in Kenya, see K. Shingledecker, *Unreached Peoples Project. Maasai Report* (Nairobi, 1982.) I do not possess at this time demographic numbers nor ecclesiastical statistics concerning the Maasai living in Tanzania.

[5] D.B. Barrett, *World Christian Encyclopaedia* (London, 1982.)

[6] Which is not always as easy as one may think. P.H. Gulliver, "The Conservative Commitment in Northern Tanzania. The Arusha and Masai," in P.H. Gulliver (ed.), *Tradition and Transition in East Africa* (London, 1969) 237: "The alleged physical distinctiveness of the Masai is likely to be somewhat illusory, being principally the result of deportment, dress and diet."

especially from European researchers.[7] We must finally point out that in 1963, a Catholic bishop resigned himself to the fact of seeing the conversion of the Maasai only within the perspective of a very distant future,[8] and that nowadays, they continue to be included among the *unreached peoples*.[9]

There exists no unanimity concerning the factors which explain this choice of the Maasai. There are different conflicting theories, one more plausible than the other, but none fully satisfactory. About fifteen years ago, we ourselves briefly treated this problem within the context of a study on a Kikuyu independent Church.[10] In a letter, Professor J. Vansina honored the paragraph which dealt with the issue in eulogistic terms, while feeling the need to conclude that the case remained partly obscure. I felt no need to contradict him since I knew that he was right. Today I wish to address the issue anew, not so much in the illusion of resolving it once and for all, but rather to see whether the harvest of studies which have appeared since then, together with the results of my own fieldwork among the people[11], would allow us to advance in the comprehension of a phenomenon which has for a long time constituted an enigma for anthropologists and a cross for missiologists.

It is true that in the course of the past few years, it has become more and more apparent that the Maasai are no longer as capable as in the past of keeping themselves from the demands formulated, and from the pressure exercised by the modern States of which they have become a part. Testimonies increase attesting to the fact that, to a certain extent, they are resigning themselves to the existing process of change. The indications concerning this participation attain henceforth a level of transparency which makes them open to becoming the

---

[7] The problem becomes more complicated by the fact that within that region, ethnic identity is a flexible and fluctuating reality. See V. Neckebrouck, *Le onzième commandement. Etiologie d'une Eglise indépendante au pied du mont Kenya* (Immensee, 1978) 43-51; V. Neckebrouck, *Le peuple affligé. Les déterminants de la fissiparité dans un nouveau mouvement religieux au Kenya Central* (Immensee, 1983) 279-281.

[8] Mgr. J. De Reeper, quoted by J. Voshaar, *Tracing God's Walking Stick in Maa* (Licence Thesis, Catholic University of Nijmegen, 1979) 278. Five years earlier, the "most optimistic" missionaries had confided to P. Julien, *Zonen van Cham.*, p. 239, that they did not anticipate any results before at least three generations.

[9] C.P. Wagner - E.R. Dayton, *Unreached Peoples* (Elgin, 1978); K. Shingledecker, *op. cit.* (1982); 1984.

[10] V. Neckebrouck, *op. cit.* (1978) 591-615.

[11] Our work among the Maasai was done from July 1978 to June 1979 and was followed by two short subsequent stays of one month each in 1985 and 1991. Prior to that, I had made a few incursions in Maasai country in the course of my first researches among the Kikuyu: 1971-1973. I had a short contact with the tribe even before that, in July 1969.

object of investigation.[12] A growing openness toward Christianity figures as one of the indicators of this new development.[13] This evolution, of which the solidity and the irreversibility still remain to be shown, nevertheless does not take away from the interest nor from the actuality of the problem here addressed. Even if it were proven that the Maasai are about to embark definitively on the path of change, the question remains why they have waited so long to make this choice. This interrogation maintains its full relevance for anthropological theory, and has lost none of its urgency and utility for missionary practice. The latter encounters similar situations elsewhere. The discovery of elements which have determined the behavior of the Maasai may thus very well hold food for thought.

---

[12] P. Hutchins, *Continuity and Change among the Maasai People* (M.A. Thesis, Fuller Theological Seminary, 1987); A. Talle, *Women at a Loss. Changes in Maasai Pastoralism and their Effects on Gender Relations* (Stockholm, 1988); M. Kituyi, *Becoming Kenyans. Socio-Economic Transformation of the Pastoral Maasai* (Nairobi, 1990.) Without being a scientific study, the work of C. Bentsen, *Maasai Days. A First-Hand Account of Life in An African Village* (London, 1990), represents an interesting testimony. Some of the changes described were certainly already in process long before, but a prejudiced image of the Maasai probably prevented for a long time researchers from seeing them or considering them worth noting.

[13] V.J. Donovan, *Christianity Rediscovered. An Epistle from the Masai* (Notre Dame, 1978); D. Priest, *Doing Theology with the Maasai* (Pasadena, 1990.) Even the baptism of a *oloiboni*, the main religious expert among the Maasai, is reported: J. Roumeguère-Eberhardt, *Les Maasai, guerriers de la savane* (Paris, 1984) 40.

4

MISSIOLOGY

It is logical to turn first to the missiologists to see how they deal with this question. Indeed, they more than anyone else are vitally concerned with the issue. From their perspective, it is not only a matter of understanding and explaining the attitude of the Maasai. The latter confronts them with another difficult dilemma: either to find the means to reorient missiological methodology so that the people comes to abandon its disaffection toward Christianity, or accept the fact that certain cultures are not open to evangelization and, consequently, that though universal by right, Christianity can not be universal in fact. In the face of the lack of success of the preaching of the Gospel among certain peoples and in certain areas of the Third World, missiology currently manifests a tendency to react with self-accusation. It attributes to missionary Christianity itself the full responsibility of the failures suffered in the non-Western world. These would find their origins in a threefold historico-structural link: the complicity of Christianity with colonial and neo-colonial politics of European powers, its solidarity with Western culture, and its association with the sectarianism of Western Christian Churches. It is assumed that the resistant peoples will ultimately be attracted by the Gospel as soon as Christians come to dissociate themselves from attitudes and behaviors of the Western nations, succeed at dissolving Christianity from the stains of being an imported religion, and show themselves capable of overcoming the arguments which divide the Churches.[14]

We cannot here undertake a minute and exhaustive critical evaluation of this etiology of refusal of Christianity. We must content ourselves with briefly advancing the reasons why in our estimation this etiology fails to explain the reaction of the Maasai. First, if the faults incriminated in the Christian mission

---

[14] This argumentation is orchestrated in a thousand and one ways in contemporary missiological literature. Often it is one or the other of these three aspects which is put to the fore, depending on the nature of the case studied, or on the personal inclinations of the author. But it may also be found presented in the more global and more systematic way as done here. See for example, H. Staffner, *The Significance of Jesus Christ in Asia* (Anand, 1985) 209-217; W. Bühlmann, *The Church of the Future. A Model for the Year 2001* (Maryknoll - Melbourne - Slough, 1986) 56.

explain the rejection of the imported religion, in which terms must we account for the behavior of the many peoples which did not hesitate to accept this religion? Would the latter have had to do with a different type of missionaries, free from the threefold link which is considered to be responsible for resistance to Christianity? More concretely, did the neighboring tribes of the Maasai benefit from the presence and actions of missionaries who were particularly enlightened and protected from the political, cultural, and confessional conditioning which would have led to the failure of their confreres among the Maasai? Might it be that the missionaries to the Chagga, the Kamba, the Meru, the Kikuyu, the Luo, the Luyha were characterized by less docility toward the colonial powers, by a less excessive attachment to Western culture, and by a more explicit ecumenical spirit than those who worked among the savanna herdsmen of the adjoining territory? The history of the evangelization of the regions inhabited by these peoples does not warrant a positive answer to these questions.[15] For example, neither the more tolerant attitude of Catholic missionaries toward the traditional Maasai culture, more particularly toward certain central institutions of this culture,[16] nor their more relaxed relations with the offices of civil power have assured them any more resounding results among the Maasai than those which their Protestant colleagues have registered.

Secondly, the missiological thesis appears to us to feed into a more subtle version of occidental ethnocentrism, i.e. that of the missiological tribe. Tributary to the anti-Western ideology of the moment, the contemporary missiological theory developed an exaggerated conscience of the errors committed in the past by the heralds of the Gospel. To restore good conscience, it freely charges them of all the sins of Israel, while failing to realize that it thus unduly aggrandizes the importance of the role accorded to missionaries in the etiology of the present religious situation of non-Western peoples. Conversely, the role of the latter in the construction of their own religious destiny is reduced to insignificance. Would not the different responses of the peoples to the missionary propagation suggest that the search for the elements which explain the success or the failure of the missionary enterprise cannot be limited to taking into consideration the nature of the missionary strategies expressed in terms of their attitude toward the political powers, toward the indigenous cultures, and toward the division of the Churches? More generally, is this exclusive focus upon the missionaries and their comportment not a refusal of the real reasons for the acceptance or the rejection of the Gospel? Is this not a considerable over-evaluation of the role and the

---

[15] See V. Neckebrouck, *op. cit.* (1978.)
[16] For example, the initiation of young girls.

importance of these missionaries, at the expense of the explanatory value of the strength and of the creativity and the initiative of those in the midst of whom they have operated? How can it be proved that the attitude of the missionaries constitutes the only variable, or even the most important variable for understanding the reaction to their preaching of the peoples of the Third World? Rather than regarding the latter as amorphic, apathic, and merely passive people, completely determined by the behavior of others, would it not be expedient to take these populations seriously and to take account of the possibility that their desires and aspirations, their stratagems and their tactical steps, their systems of values and of symbols, the structures of their societies and their modes of production, and the ups and downs of their historical development have determined their reaction to the new religious message? May the desire of Africans to embrace Christianity or their decision to reject it be put solely on the account of the behavior of a handful of European missionaries? Or could it be that the attitude toward Christianity proceeds essentially and principally from the peoples themselves and constitutes for them a response destined to fulfil a certain aspiration, an attempt to resolve a dilemma, an effort to bring an end to an interrogation, a discomfort or a tension which they experience? Is it not a little naive to believe that the Gospel has been massively accepted in certain regions for the sake of pleasing the missionary (lets say to thank him for willingly distantiating himself from his fellow countrymen, from his culture, and from the schismatic past of his Church) and has been just as massively rejected in other regions to obstruct this missionary by punishing him for what contemporary missiology considers to be his principal stains? Would it not be more pertinent to grant the Africans their own reasons for acting in a particular way, their own motivations rooted in the order, the structures, the dynamics and the dialectics penetrating and determining their societies, their cultures and their histories? Would it not be that it is in searching in this direction that a scientific missiology may come to replace a discourse based upon a premise of which, until further notice, the only merit consists of coinciding with certain fashionable tastes? The missiological argumentation concerns important themes relating to missionary historiography and methodology. Nevertheless, as an explanation for the reaction of non-Western peoples, it reflects the contemporary Western sentiments toward mission rather than the results of an objective investigation of historical and anthropological facts advanced by the field itself.

The refusal of the imported religion constitutes only one aspect of a more global attitude of the Maasai, which are often quoted as the example par excellence of what has been habitually referred to as the conservatism of the pastoral peoples of East Africa. The stereotypical image of the Maasai is that of a people solidly attached to its way of life, its structures and traditional values, hermetically closed to all intrusion, not only of the religion coming from the West, but of all Western cultural influence.[17] K. King certainly attracted attention to the fact that a certain number of Maasai have, from the beginning of the colonization, participated in modernistic nationalistic activities, and have shown themselves to be interested in Western education. But it must be said that these individuals constituted only a tiny minority, without influence on the masses of the people and whose attitudes and initiatives do not substantially modify the image of an ethnic group clearly engaged in a conservative option.[18] Hence, the negative response of the Maasai to the evangelizing efforts may and must be seen, at least basically, as a particular symptom of a much more general and global phenomenon, notably the radical opposition of the people to every form of socio-cultural change under the auspices of the West. The column of the 'faits divers' of missionary history is a decidedly too narrow basis upon which to build such a massive edifice. Moreover, the Maasai tradition ignores any distinction between religion and the rest of culture. For these Nilotic pastoralists, Christianity was first and foremost 'one of these foreign things' which was supposed to be ignored as were other foreign imports.

It is thus not surprising that the question of the indifference of the Maasai toward Christianity has thusfar invariably been envisioned from a global perspective. In spite of the fact that some have underlined that religion constitutes the preponderant structure in East-African pastoral societies and plays a dominant role in their functioning[19], almost no attention has been paid to this religion itself as the possible source of the religious conservatism of the Maasai. As we shall see, as soon as the religious aspects are taken into account in this context, it is only from a Marxist point of view, as superstructural expressions of determining economic conditions. Relegating to later the effort to examine whether religious anthropology would not be able to offer a more original and more substantial contribution to the debate, in this article we have decided to work within the frame of the general global perspective.

---

[17] W.R. Hotchkiss, *Then and Now in Kenya Colony* (New York, 1937) "The Masai have resisted *all efforts* towards their regeneration." E. Huxley, *The Sorcerer's Apprentice* (London, 1949) 89, speaks of "these obstinately conservative nomads" who "seem like dinosaurs or pterodactyls, survivors from a past age with a dying set of values, aristocratic, manly, free, doomed. Like everything else *in nature that will not or cannot conform to a changed environment*, they must perish or merge." Italics ours.

[18] K. King, "The Kenya Masai and the Protest Phenomenon 1900-1960," *Journal of African History* (1971.)

[19] P. Bonte, "Cattle for God: An Attempt at a Marxist Analysis of the Religion of East African Herdsmen," *Social Compass* (1975.)

NOMADISM

By way of transition, let us first take into account a thesis which, while presenting itself as a concrete application of current missiological theory, appeals to an absolutely primordial and central aspect of the Maasai culture. As such, it acquires a global significance and, because of this, has lent itself to explain not only the religious conservatism of the Maasai, but Maasai conservatism in general. This cultural trait, deriving from the very mode of existence of the people and expressing the way in which it situates itself with regard to space, is nomadism. In the minds of most Westerners, the concepts of civilization and development are, both in their origins and in their further development, inseparably associated with sedentarization, i.e. with the principle of territorial organization as opposed to that of perpetual mobility which governs the nomadic universe.[20] If, as believed by Ibn Khaldoun in the fourteenth century, the nomadic way of life protects the people who adopt it against the degeneration and the 'decadence' of the 'civilized' life of farmers and sedentary townsmen[21], it by the same token prevents them from access to it. With body and soul attached to 'civilization,' Christianity organized its structures on the basis of the territorial principle: parishes, dioceses, archdioceses, patriarchates, etc., are territorially delineated. Having been unwilling or unable to move away from these particular civilizational structures, the Church could only witness to the failure of its efforts to penetrate a society ignorant of the territorial principle.[22] Just as a Western culture based on the sedentary premise has had to find itself reduced to powerlessness.

---

[20] We may wonder whether this ancient and profoundly rooted prejudice is not bound to disappear in modern industrial society. J. Roumeguere-Eberhardt, *op. cit.*, p. 30, writes that the way in which the Maasai move in function of the livestock "exige une mobilité comparable à celle imposée par les contraintes de nos sociétés industrielles."

[21] Cfr. M. d'Hertefelt, *Political Anthropology* (Leuven, 1990) 128-129.

[22] The thesis has been defended by, for example, J. Dempsey, *Mission on the Nile* (London, 1955.) It was reiterated by A. Shorter at the occasion of a Round Table in the course of a colloquium on the Universality of Christianity (Louvain, feb. 21 and 22, 1991.)

We may easily acknowledge that, in principle, the sedentary character of a population presents certain facilities for the evangelizing work exercised by a Church with territorial organizational structures. The fact remains that the sedentary societies which, despite long and obstinate efforts toward their evangelization, have not embraced Christianity are legion in the world. Moreover, the extreme mobility of the Gypsies has not prevented them from becoming Catholic, Protestant, or Pentecostal. The simple reminder of these elementary facts suffices to show that the argument does not possess conclusive explanatory value in and of itself.

AN UNFORTUNATE EXPERIENCE

A certain number of our older informants explain and justify the conservatism of their people in pointing out the rather deplorable state of the small minority who showed sympathy to Western and Christian civilization to which K. King refers. The people have been able to observe where deviation from tradition led those who had been directed along this path. In fact, throughout the colonial period, there was not the least indication that the education offered by the missions or the participation in other modern areas provided those who engaged in them any social promotion or economic advantages whatsoever in comparison with those who had remained faithful to traditional orthopraxis.[23] On the contrary, everything seemed to indicate that modernization concurred with the impoverishment of its adherents. The state of poverty to which the Christian Maasai were reduced constituted a terrifying example for the other members of the tribe. The biography of Molonket Olokorinya Ole Sempele, one of the typical representatives of the group in question, is instructive in this regard. This very gifted and dynamic man ended up losing the rather high social status which he possessed in traditional society without being able to find the equivalent in the modern environment.[24] In his youth, Sempele far from lacked material resources. He possessed a numerous flock and, in 1909, had been able to buy himself a trip to America.[25] The image of him which Mrs. Stauffacher paints in 1930, two decades later, is completely different. It is one of total deprivation and destitution: "They are about the poorest folks on the place, have no cattle at all only garden stuffs – Others give them things – like milk and they have a few chickens – No one seems to know what he has done with his property for he had a lot at one time."[26] The Maasai threw the blame for the impoverishment

---

[23] Cfr. K. King, *art. cit.* (1971) 137.

[24] K. King, *A Biography of Molonket Olokorinya Ole Sempele*, in: K. King - A. Salim (eds.), *Kenya Historical Biographies* (Nairobi, 1971 a); V. Neckebrouck, *op. cit.* (1978) 529-539.

[25] K. King, *African Students in the American Negro College. Some Notes on the "Good African"* (Phylon, 1970); K. King, *art. cit.* (1971 a.)

[26] Letter quoted by K. King, *art. cit.* (1971 a) 22.

of their converted and modernist brothers on the fact that they had departed from the ways paved by tradition. Often this idea is internalized by the victims of modernization themselves.[27] In the eyes of the people, the misfortune of the pauperized progressive Maasai only led to prove the correctness of its own traditionalist and conservative option. It confirmed its attitude of resistance to all change instigated by white men who had brought upon the tribe nothing but one calamity after the other.

Of course, one may reverse the argument by stating that the sad fate of the progressive Maasai was the *consequence* of the traditionalist mentality of an overwhelming majority of the people, rather than its *cause*. In a society generally opposed to change, modernists are almost fatally condemned to failure precisely because one remains indifferent or hostile to their enterprises and, a priori, neither their efforts nor their realizations are acknowledged or valued. This is why we have been able to explain, at least partly, the success of the modernist Kikuyu elite as well as the failure of the modernist Maasai elite by linking both to the different basic attitudes toward socio-cultural change of their respective peoples.[28] Moreover, my interlocutors remained mute when I pointed out that the modernists were far from the only Maasai proletarians. But that is not the issue. It matters here to become aware, beyond any objective reality, of the collective thought of the people and of the way in which they justify their options. The fact that this thought misses logical rigor, reasons in vicious circles, and betrays subjective rationalizations does not subtract from its impact on the minds, and thereby on the events and the course of history. In sum, while acknowledging the minor explanatory value of the argument, it is necessary to mainly underline its essential limits.

---

[27] The Maasai writer H. Ole Kulet turned this theme into one of the central ideas of his second novel: H. Ole Kulet, *To Become a Man* (Nairobi, 1972.) See especially pp. 129-130.

[28] V. Neckebrouck, *op. cit.* (1978) 529-539.

PROSPERITY

Some see in the conservatism of the Maasai a direct consequence of their material wealth and prosperity. The people are considered to be probably the richest tribe of Africa, both in landed property and in livestock. Many less wealthy people were forced to insert themselves in the modern circuit so as to obtain the cash necessary to satisfy the tax demands of the colonial government. The Maasai were protected against this constraint, which has modernization as its corollary, by their excellent economic situation. This would have inhibited every movement toward change.[29]

This thesis seems to presuppose that wealth and prosperity necessarily lead people to close themselves to acculturation. To us, this hypothesis seems unproved. Of course, material well-being may constitute a protection against change. But it plays this role of protection only in as far as the peoples concerned are willing to effectively use it to this end. Economic prosperity may function as a support which assures the viability of conservatism. Without it, the conservatism of the Arusha, a people geographically near and culturally related to the Maasai, has been forced, willy-nilly, to compromise with the enemy.[30] It thus constitutes a condition which renders maintaining the conservative option infinitely easier. But it does not automatically explain this option itself. There are countries in Africa where it is precisely the groups which are most well off from the material point of view who were the first to open themselves to modernist influences. If during the colonial epoch the Maasai constituted the wealthiest ethnic group of Tanzania and Kenya, why was the evolution different in these countries? The thesis thus does not resolve the problem. It moreover triggers other questions. What about the wealth of the Maasai? And mainly, to what

---

[29] See, for example, G.H. Mungeam, "Masai and Kikuyu Responses to the Establishment of Administration in the East Africa Protectorate," *Journal of African History* (1970.) Without referring to the Maasai in particular, H. Maurier, "Religions africaines: les pasteurs," *Vivant Univers*, nr° 356 (1985) 36-37, notes that nomadic tribes show indifference to Western and missionary offers as long as they themselves are prosperous.

[30] See V. Neckebrouck, *op. cit.* (1978) 582-590.

extent did its particular nature allow it to act in the specific circumstances of the colonial situation as a barrier against acculturation?

It must be said that the Maasai may be counted amongst the richer pastoral peoples of Africa. In 1930 the volume of the herd of an average family was estimated at seventy-five head of cattle, eighty-five sheep and goats and eighteen donkeys.[31] Another source mentions for the same period twenty-five heads of cattle per person.[32] For the period starting from 1950, Jacobs estimates the herd of a typical Maasai family (eight to ten persons) to be one hundred twenty five to one hundred forty heads of cattle, one hundred fifty to two hundred heads of goat and sheep, and at least five to six donkeys.[33] Nevertheless, as we mention these numbers which are impressive at first sight, we must not forget to specify that this relatively high number of animals was absolutely necessary to allow the herdsmen of the Rift Valley to survive the periodic draughts which time and again decimated their flocks.[34] In the condition in which the Maasai live, cattle constitutes a fragile form of wealth, highly perishable. At each moment the animals are exposed to being devoured by big game, to the risk of loss, theft, and raids, to decimation due to draught and epizootics. The wealth of the pastoralists thus reveals itself largely an illusion. Historical research shows that in comparison with many other regions the importance of the pastoral way of life in the production of deprived people constitutes a distinctive characteristic of poverty in Africa.[35] It must be added that the living capital of the Maasai was not easily converted to money. Severe government restrictions had imposed permanent quarantine on Maasai livestock. Outside the reserve, the cattle could be sold only to be slain. Fearing the competition of the Maasai on the cattle market, the colonists had procured the imposition of this measure, under the pretext that their own flock would be contaminated if they came in contact with the animals of African owners which were believed to be affected by diseases. The only market accessible to the Maasai was from then on the Nairobi slaughterhouse, which could be reached only by crossing a zone infested with the tsé-tsé fly. A large number of animals regularly died on the way. Those which survived the crossing arrived weakened and thin, which conveniently allowed the buyers to lower the prices. It is also true that the Maasai traditionally covered an

---

[31] G.W. Huntingford, *The Southern Nilo-Hamites* (London, 1953) 107.

[32] J.B. Orr - F.R. Gilks, *The Physique and Health of Two African Tribes* (London, 1931.)

[33] A. Jacobs, "Maasai Pastoralism in Historical Perspective," T. Monod (ed.), *Pastoralism in Tropical Africa* (London, 1975) 408.

[34] R.D. Waller, *The Lords of East Africa: The Maasai in the Mid-Nineteenth Century (1840-1885)* (Ph.D. Dissertation, University of Cambridge, 1978) 61-62.

[35] J. Iliffe, *The African Poor. A History* (Cambridge, 1987) 65-81.

immense territory of rich grazing grounds. But it must not be forgotten that in the beginning of the century they were forced to abandon their best pastures – the center of the Rift Valley, the plateaus of Mau, Laikipia and Uasin Gishu, the plains of Kapitir and the region of Donyo Sabuk.[36] The reserve which was given to them in exchange was not only considerably smaller in surface, but proved to be much less fertile and much less regularly watered by the rains. Certain regions were almost unlivable because they were too dry or occupied by flies which transmitted fatal diseases. The harsh reduction of the tribal territory led to the destruction of the ecological balance. The flocks had become too numerous to be adequately supported by a soil which ended up exposed to erosion by permanent frequentation. We may add to this that, beginning in the twenties, the Maasai were forced to pay almost double the taxes imposed upon other African people (for example twenty instead of twelve or sixteen shillings elsewhere) precisely because of their supposed wealth.[37] In reality, as was pointed out by R.L. Tignor, it was difficult for the Maasai to procure the money necessary to pay the tax. At certain times they were even totally incapable of satisfying the fiscal demands.[38] In sum, we have good reason to believe that the fiscal exigencies of the government weighed just as heavily on the Maasai as on the other tribes. No less than their neighbors, they were subjected to an economic pressure which should normally have led to a shaking of the traditional structures and way of life, and to an openness toward innovation and change.

---

[36] See V. Neckebrouck, *op. cit.* (1978) 531-532.

[37] L. James, "The Kenya Masai. A Nomadic People under Modern Administration," *Africa. Journal of the International African Institute* (1939.)

[38] R.L. Tignor, "The Maasai Warriors: Pattern Maintenance and Violence in Colonial Kenya," *Journal of African History* (1972) 273.

ISOLATION

Another theory explains the Maasai conservatism by the fact that the people would have been deliberately isolated from the forces of change by a paternalizing colonizer. It is said that the latter would have tried to keep the tribe in the state in which it had been found because it was considered an eminent representative of the 'good savage' which he would have been interested in preserving intact.[39] This thesis is especially held by acculturated Maasai.[40] It is said that the Maasai reserve was declared to be an inaccessible zone and that non-Maasai were allowed to penetrate this territory only when granted special permission. It is also argued that the ministry of education was not disposed to dispense to the Maasai the same Westernizing education which was provided for the other tribes. In our opinion, this reasoning is rooted mainly in the resentment and embarrassment of certain acculturated Maasai who profoundly condemn

---

[39] The perception of the Maasai as eminent representative of the "noble savage" was not cultivated by the British only. Here are the terms in which the French Spiritan missionary A. Le Roy, *op. cit.*, p. 408-409, expressed himself: "Je regarde, et, bien certainement, j'admire. Voilà donc enfin d'authentiques sauvages, tels qu'on n'en vit jamais dans les champs de foire, de vrais représentants de cette race que Thomson, avec raison, a appelée la plus belle, la plus extraordinaire d'Afrique. Elle fait, sans doute, la terreur de toutes les tribus environnantes; mais, en voyant ces formes superbes, ce port académique, cette fierté, cette distinction, ces manières, on se rappelle involontairement la parole de saint Grégoire le Grand: 'Quel dommage que ces hommes ne soient pas chrétiens'!" Nevertheless, it never was the intention of Le Roy to preserve the Maasai as they were.

[40] Tepilit Ole Saitoti, *Maasai* (London, 1980) 272. The thesis was exposed to us with much conviction in 1973 by John Tompo Ole Mpaayei, at the time General Secretary of the Bible Society of Kenya. Some Europeans, however, equally adhere to this explanation. See, for example, J. Roberts, *A Land Full of People. Kenya Today* (London, 1967) 48.

the past resistance of their people and who wish at all costs to attribute the responsibility for it to a deliberate initiative of the colonizer.[41]

The argument does not resist the facts. If it is true that a special permission was required to enter the Maasai reserve, this measure was not inspired by the desire to preserve the cultural virginity of the Maasai inviolated, but for fear of their militarism which throughout the colonial period the British have not ceased to dread. As far as education is concerned, all literature, based both on interviews with African participants and on archival sources and accounts of Europeans, attests to the fact that the Maasai have always violently opposed the efforts of the administration to invite or even force them to send their children to school.[42] Several administrators of the Maasai districts have consecrated the best of their time and energy to direct the Maasai toward the schools and also to induce them by argumentation, persuasion, kindness, prudence, ruse, threat, and force to receive favorably other innovations, notably in the area of stock-breeding. It is thus incorrect to pretend that the Maasai were deliberately isolated from all danger of acculturation. Other pastoral peoples of East Africa lived a nomadic life very far from the centers of administration and commercial activity. This factor could be invoked as an element of explanation of their traditionalism. However, for the Maasai, the argument of the geographical distance from the agents of westernization cannot be maintained, since they live in the neighborhood of Nairobi and of the White Highlands.

A theory has been proposed which may pass as a variation of the preceding one. According to this thesis, the absence of change among the Maasai during the twentieth century, as also among the other pastoral peoples living in the vast, semi-barren countries of Kenya and Uganda in general, constitutes the

---

[41] The Maasai in his traditional dress and smeared with red ochre is nowadays exposed to the mockery, not so much of Europeans as of his own African fellow countrymen who profoundly despise him and accuse him of being a primitive, a savage, and even a beast. We have often been disheartened in witnessing to the humiliating, vexing, and inhuman treatment which Kikuyu, Kamba, Chagga or other Africans inflict upon the Maasai as soon as the latter leave their tribal territory. Cfr. R.A. Levine - D.T. Campbell, *Ethnocentrism: Theories of Conflict, Ethnic Attitudes and Group Behavior* (New York - London, 1972) 195: "In a 1965 survey organized by the authors, the Masai were most frequently mentioned by other Kenya groups as being not only the most backward and uncivilized but also the most dirty and stupid."

[42] On the few exceptions to this rule, see V. Neckebrouck, *op. cit.*, 1978, p. 591, 529-539. R.L. Tignor, *The Colonial Transformation of Kenya. The Kamba, Kikuyu and Maasai from 1900 to 1939* (Princeton, 1976) 286-287: "There can be no question that the primary responsibility for the educational lag of the Maasai cannot be laid at the feet of the colonial rulers."

consequence of an economic choice made by the European masters.[43] Through-out the colonial period, the governments of these two countries were interested only in agricultural production and, after the Second World War, in the development of secondary industries. As a result of this agricultural and industrial orientation assigned to the process of change, financial and administrative resources, which were limited from the outset, were refused the pastoral nomads. At no time and in none of the two countries did the colonizer think of elaborating a policy of exploiting the potential represented by cattle-raising in the regions inhabited by these peoples. From the beginning of the century, the dominant preoccupation of the successive governments which dealt with the nomadic or semi-nomadic groups was to pacify them and to have law and order reign in the territories. In this regard, one of the major problems which they had to confront was the intensive practice of cattle raids in which the pastoralists indulged. It is the desire to put an end to these raids, as well as that of submitting an erring people to more efficient control, which drove the governments to enclose the nomads within tribal boundaries and to declare the zones which they inhabited 'closed districts.' Besides these elementary administrative measures and the deploying of the military and police forces necessary to maintain the *Pax Britannica*, the colonizer barely intervened in the life of the nomads. All the more so because the white colonists feared the competition of African pastoralists and had declared themselves hostile to the development of indigenous stock-raising. As a result, the administration chose to ignore the livestock of the autochthonous population as a potential source of prosperity, except in as far as the confiscation of the animals was regarded as a sanction suitable for the infringements on the colonial rule, and as far as the wealth in animals functioned as a basis for the calculation of taxation. So as to allow the rise of prospering cooperatives thereby insuring the commercialization of the products from European cattle-breeding[44], the stock of the Maasai needed to be put in quarantine and could only little by little have access to the markets. In sum, a positive economic policy with respect to the pastoralists was totally nonexistent. On the contrary, attempts were made to discourage pastoral life. And most of all, no money was spent on the development of the areas inhabited by the nomads who constituted a permanent threat to both the *Pax Britannica* and European stock-breeding. The authors conclude that the colonizer did not have the concern to mobilize the potential toward change inherent in pastoral societies. If these societies have remained virtually

---

[43] R. Van Zwanenberg - A. King, *An Economic History of Kenya and Uganda 1800-1970* (Nairobi, 1975) 87-97; I.R. Spencer, "Pastoralism and Colonial Policy in Kenya, 1895-1929," in: R.I. Rotberg (ed.), *Colonialism and Hunger: East and Central Africa* (Massachusetts - Toronto, 1983.)

[44] Such as the *Kenya Meat Commission* and the *Creameries Cooperative of Kenya*.

19

unchanged for a century, the blame is on the colonial government which failed to take the initiatives necessary to stimulate economic and cultural evolution.

This is not the place to submit this theory to a detailed examination. It suffices to highlight the most striking weaknesses. The authors argue that little money was invested in the reserves of pastoral people toward the transformation of the prevailing way of life. But isn't this also the case for the Kikuyu reserves? Haven't the colonists, there too, tried to avoid change and the amelioration of the conditions of life so as to insure the flow of emigrant workers from the reserves? They invoke the agricultural and industrial orientation of the colonial economic set-up. But wasn't it essentially the agricultural economy of the colonists that they tried to protect, if we remember that the African agriculturalists were denied the right to modernize and to diversify their traditional economy? Didn't the quasi-totality of the subsidies granted to agriculture go to European agriculture? They hold that the possibilities of the African pastoral economy have been sacrificed for the European stock-raising. But wasn't in the same way and for the same reasons the development of the Kikuyu agricultural economy neglected and radically blocked? Isn't it precisely there that the core of the conflict between the Kikuyu and the colonial regime lies?[45] They point to an absence of preoccupation with modernization of the administration in its relations with the pastoral people. To this argument, we already have answered by criticizing the preceding thesis: there have been considerable efforts on the part of the administration to launch the Maasai on the path of socio-cultural change and acculturation, but the Maasai have resisted these attempts. We will return to this point. For the time being it is enough to state that this resistance sheds light on what in our eyes constitutes the main lacuna in the thesis we discuss. At no point do the authors allow the opinion and the attitude of the Maasai themselves to come to the fore, as if change constitutes a process which unfolds in the total absence of African participants. These people thus find themselves reduced to puppets, content with undergoing the decisions which are made on their account by European agents. Hence, in the acceptance or refusal of socio-cultural change, the African factor would be considered a merely subsidiary and inconsistent variable. Acculturation or its rejection is the fruit of interaction between all the components of the human landscape. It is important to study the interrelations between these, and to circumscribe their respective contributions to the option for or against modernization which results from this game of interaction. The analyses of the above authors do not even teach us whether or not the Maasai considered change a desirable alternative. A fortiori, they remain mute on the ulterior questions relating to the motives of the Maasai choice.

---

[45] Cfr. V. Neckebrouck, *op. cit.* (1978) 561-581.

THE MILITARY ORDEAL

The Maasai keep the memory of a prophet who predicted that the Europeans would destroy the larger part of the tribe if they would venture a rebellion.[46] Some have attached great importance for the understanding of Maasai conservatism to the fact that the people have succeeded in avoiding all military confrontation of any significant scale with the government armed forces.[47] It is said that by making the defeated people lose confidence in their institutions and traditional values a decisive military defeat prepares the way for acculturation. Conversely, the absence of military trauma would allow for the preservation of unshaken faith in the tested ways of tradition.[48] For example, it has been described how the initial ferocious resistance of the Nandi to the invader was replaced by a receptivity toward his culture once the colonial army had delivered the final blow to the warriors of the tribe.[49]

---

[46] N. Leys, *Kenya* (London, 1924) 108.

[47] A. Meister, *L'Afrique peut-elle partir? Changement social et développement en Afrique Orientale* (Paris, 1966) 27, propagates an opinion completely contrary to the facts according to which the Maasai have been "the only tribe which offers armed resistance to the European conquerors." This myth holds a double error. First, it ignores the armed resistance of a large number of Kenyan tribes to the British occupation. There are indeed few ethnic groups of the country who have not had the experience of military confrontation with the Europeans. (For a selective bibliography on this subject, see V. Neckebrouck, *op. cit.* (1978) 110-111.) On the other hand, one of the tribes of which the armed resistance has been rather limited, or non-existent, is precisely that of the Maasai (Cfr. *Ibidem).* The historical truth is thus the exact opposite of that which Meister points out.

[48] G.R. Sandford, *An Administrative and Political History of the Masai Reserve* (London, 1919) 2; G.H. Mungeam, *British Rule in Kenya, 1895-1912: The Establishment of Administration in the East Africa Protectorate* (Oxford, 1966) 129-132.

[49] S. Arap Ngey, *Nandi Resistance to the Establishment of British Administration* (Hadith II, 1970); P. Mwaura, *The Battle of Armageddon,* Inside Kenya Today, 1971; A.T. Matson, *Nandi Resistance to British Rule* (Nairobi, 1972.)

Nevertheless, considering among others the case of the Arusha[50], one may argue that it happens that a military defeat confirms rather than erodes the attachment to traditional values. From the point of view of effects, military breakdown is comparable to the state of crisis caused by famine, epidemics, epizootics, or other similar calamities. Such afflictions do not provoke either identical or homogenous responses. They are susceptible to making people turn away from the tribal religion, but they may also bring about a revival of fidelity to the tradition, or even the return of converted Christians to their former religion.[51] Moreover, the fact that the Maasai have been able to avoid a decisive armed conflict with the colonial forces does not mean that they had no idea of British military power. On the contrary, in participating along with the English in a number of punitive expeditions, they were perfectly informed about the capacity of the colonial army and sufficiently aware of their own impotence with regard to the British. It is not necessary to have actually experienced defeat or to have even measured oneself tangibly against the enemy in order to realize that one is outmatched and to admit defeat. There are certain events which, though not taking place on the battlefield, nevertheless possess a psychological significance which is identical to that attributed to a military defeat and which are capable of discrediting, as surely as such a defeat, the traditional system in the eyes of the participants. The treaties of 1904 and 1911, which the Maasai have endorsed because they knew that armed resistance was useless, have certainly acquired this meaning. And in reality, they were worth the worst military mishaps.[52]

---

[50] P.H. Gulliver, "The Evolution of Arusha Trade," in P. Bohannan - G. Dalton (eds.), *Markets in Africa* (Evanston, 1962); P.H. Gulliver, *Social Control in an African Society. A Study of the Arusha, Agricultural Masai of Northern Tanganyika* (London, 1963); P.H. Gulliver, "The Conservative Commitment in Northern Tanganyika: The Arusha and Masai," in P.H. Gulliver (ed.), *Tradition and Transition in East Africa* (Berkeley, 1969.) Cfr. V. Neckebrouck, *op. cit.* (1978) 582-591.

[51] See, for example, M. Mainga, "A History of Lozi Religion to the End of the Nineteenth Century," in T.O. Ranger - I. Kimambo (eds.), *The Historical Study of African Religion* (London, 1972) 103; T.O. Ranger, "The Role of Ndebele and Shona Religious Authorities in the Rebellions of 1896 and 1897," in E. Stokes - R. Brown (eds.), *The Zambezian Past* (Manchester, 1966) 96; T.O. Ranger, "The Churches, the Nationalist State and African Religion," in E. Fashole-Luke (ed.), *Christianity in Independent Africa* (London, 1978) 499; H. Bucher, *Spirits and Power: An Analysis of Shona Cosmology* (Cape Town, 1980) 134; D. Kooiman, "Change of Religion as a Way to Survival. Some Source Material from 19th - Century Travancore, India," in P. Quarles van Ufford - M. Schoffeleers (eds.), *Religion and Development. Towards an Integrated Approach* (Amsterdam, 1988.)

[52] Cfr. R.L. Tignor, *art. cit.*, p. 274-275. It is on the basis of these treaties that the Maasai were forced to abandon to the white colonists enormous stretches of land which constituted their most fertile grazing grounds.

AN INNATE MENTALITY

Another attempt to give account of the Maasai conservatism consists of bringing it back to a particular trait of the psychological physiognomy of the people and of the pastoral peoples in general. The Maasai are imbued with their own superiority and that of their culture. All the other peoples, Africans or other, are apprehended by them as not only different, but also as essentially inferior. A people which is to such a degree conscious of its own value and that of its way of life will be little inclined to fertilization by contributions coming from societies and cultures for which it finally feels nothing but indifference and despise. According to this theory, conservatism and resistance to change would be inherent in the Maasai mentality.[53]

It is certainly true that the Maasai were and still are largely characterized by the traits which this thesis attributes to them.[54] However, even a strong degree of ethnocentrism is not incompatible with a more or less large openness toward the stranger. The ethnocentric reflex is universal and may just as well accompany a progressive comportment as a conservative choice. Openness to change does not necessarily imply depreciation of the past or inferiorization of one's own culture.[55] If the Maasai consider themselves to be superior to their neighbors, the latter, *while being involved in acculturation*, did pay them back![56]

---

[53] H.K. Schneider, "Pokot Resistance to Change," in W.R. Bascom - M.J. Herskovits (eds.), *Continuity and Change in African Cultures* (Chicago, 1959); P.H. Gulliver, *art. cit.* (1969) 234; S. Ole Saibull - R. Carr, *Herd and Spear. The Maasai of East Africa* (London, 1981) 20.

[54] The Maasai are not ignorant of their depreciation by the neighboring peoples (see note 41) which is based upon an evaluation in modern economic, social, and cultural terms. Nevertheless, as shown in the survey of R.A. Levine - D.T. Campbell, *op. cit.*, p. 195, they refuse to internalize it and, on the contrary, continue to regard themselves as superior. This attitude is possible only because of a reduction of the dissonance between auto-perception and external evaluation, obtained by means of a rigorous adhesion to the traditional categories of appreciation, that is to say those of a warrior pastoral civilization.

[55] V. Neckebrouck, *L'Afrique Noire et la crise religieuse de l'Occident* (Tabora, 1971) 125-127; F. Braudel, *Grammaire des civilisations* (Paris, 1988) 38.

[56] Cfr. note 41.

23

P.H. Gulliver himself, who belongs to those who invoke the conservative temperament of the Maasai, admits that "despite their seemingly implacable attitude and evaluation of others, the Masai have for several generations recruited and accepted non-Masai into their communities."[57] I add that this openness manifests itself not only toward foreign people, but also toward certain elements of the foreign culture. Thus, to mention only one example, it seems more and more plausible that the origin and the development of the central religious institution of the Maasai, that of the *oloiboni* or prophet, are due to Kikuyu and Kalenjin influence.[58] The question is to know why this drive toward assimilation ceased when confronted with the Western tide.

Even in abstracting from these facts, which clearly contradict the thesis, it is too easy to content oneself with explaining the conservative reflex through ... the conservative mentality itself. Such an explanation constitutes a tautology. One does not advance the comprehension of the refusal of Hindus to kill cows, even in a period of famine, by saying that the Hindu is conservative or filled with a sense of the superiority of his own way of acting. Such reasoning postulates that progressive options possess the monopoly of rationality and that conservative choices are necessarily acts of submission to a blind instinct, deprived of all intelligible motivation and of all rational justification. In the presence of a conservative reaction, of the rejection of change, one may thus save oneself the trouble of researching the underlying motives which accord consistency and intelligibility to the adopted attitude. I believe to have shown, on the contrary, concerning the attachment of the Kikuyu to the circumcision of girls, that by digging a little deeper, it is possible to discover a logic which is just as consistent and consequential as the one which is believed to govern progressive comportment.[59] Consequently, it is important to discover precisely which traditional values undergird the conservative option of the Maasai, wherein they are rooted, and why they remain attached to them.

We could show that the reasoning implied in the thesis is tautological in still another way. The conservative reaction of the Maasai is explained by invoking their conservative mentality, according to the adage *Agere sequitur esse*. But doesn't this argument imply an understanding of the mentality which represents it as a static entity which would constitute the product of a biological structure and would therefore find itself inscribed and programmed in physical nature,

---

[57] P.H. Gulliver, *art. cit.* (1969) 237.

[58] See J.L. Berntsen, *Pastoralism, Raiding and Prophets: Maasailand in the Nineteenth Century* (Doctoral Thesis, University of Wisconsin, 1979) 121-128.

[59] V. Neckebrouck, *op. cit.* (1978) 295, 373-400.

participating as such in its relative stability and immutability? Would it not be more appropriate to see it as primarily the fruit of a historical situation, of a sociological and cultural context? Moreover, this situation and this context of which the mentality constitutes in part the result and the reflection are, far from remaining unchanged, subjected to transformations and susceptible to evolution. Being nourished by them, the mentality finds itself carried along by this movement. It then appears as a reality which is essentially dynamic, open, and evolving to the rhythm of historical, sociological, and cultural transformations which societies undergo. The supposed own character of the Maasai mentality would thus not constitute a solution to the problem of the people's resistance to change. The question which must be resolved is precisely that of knowing *why* the Maasai mentality has not evolved in the midst of a new historical and sociological environment. The thesis has transformed into an answer precisely that which needs to be explained.[60]

---

[60] The argument concerning the tautological nature of this thesis, developed in our study of 1978, p. 597-598, has since been reiterated by P. Rigby, *Persistent Pastoralists. Nomadic Societies in Transition* (London, 1985) 95.

UNADAPTED ACCULTURATION

The tautological pitfall can also be discerned in the theory of R.S. Merrill for whom the Maasai resistance seems to be a consequence of the unadapted nature of the approach to acculturation of the administration in the Maasai reserves.[61] According to the author, the colonizer did not succeed in offering an economic alternative which was valuable and appealing to the Maasai. In particular, the imported system of education was completely unadapted to the needs of the herdsmen. Rather than serving their pastoral interest, it seemed, on the contrary, to seek to alienate them from it. As such, it was constantly in contradiction with the central cultural values of the people.

We admit that, on the whole, the facts advanced are correct. But we nevertheless cannot subscribe to the theory. In fact, in the majority of cases the Africans have resisted the first efforts of the missionaries to provide education for the children. And this almost invariably because of the same reason: it was felt that the time spent in school was lost time since one could not see the use of a Western education for the formation of a man or woman in terms of the criteria operating in traditional society. Nevertheless, in the overwhelming majority of cases, the Africans have come back from this initial negative attitude. And yet, it would not be difficult to show that this teaching entered almost always and everywhere into conflict with the ideals and exigencies of traditional societies, be they pastoral, agricultural, hunting, or fishing societies. Moreover, certain peoples even reacted against the efforts of the Europeans to render the teaching more adapted to the real situation and the concrete needs of the traditional society on the way to transformation.[62] Why did the Maasai react so

---

[61] R.S. Merrill, *Resistance to Economic Change* (Proceedings of the Minnesota Academy of Science, 1960.) This thesis is not a useless repetition of that of isolation. The latter attributes to the colonial government a deliberate policy of preservation of the Maasai from the instances of acculturation, while the former insists upon the unadapted character of the acculturation made available.

[62] The Kikuyu, neighbors of the Maasai, constitute one of the best examples of this type of reaction. Cfr. V. Neckebrouck, *op. cit.* (1978) 186-207.

differently than other peoples? Why, with them, was the initial resistance prolonged during the whole colonial period and beyond? The author offers hardly
any answers to these questions. Rather than explaining the Maasai resistance,
his argumentation in fact amounts to reaffirming it in a different, but at that no
less problematic way.

THE ECOLOGICAL ARGUMENT

According to P.H. Gulliver, the determining factor for understanding Maasai conservatism resides in the particular constellation of their physical environment.[63] The semi-nomadic Maasai dwell in a country the grazing grounds of which are dotted with stretches of unfertile land, with regions lacking water pools, and bush infested with the tsé-tsé fly. The places where one might resupply oneself with water are dispersed often very far one from the other. For the whole of the territory, the rainfall is sufficient only once every six or seven years. If we leave out the heart of the Rift Valley and the plateau of Laikipia, from where the Maasai have in fact been expelled, agriculture can be practised only here and there, in certain places which are privileged and isolated one from the other. The population is accustomed to living under the threat of devastating draught which strikes the region at regular intervals and of which tradition retains a terrifying memory. In this harsh environment which puts human endurance to a difficult test, the Maasai have nevertheless succeeded in maintaining themselves as rich and prosperous herdsmen according to African criteria. Still, they have maintained a keen awareness of the essential frailty of their material well-being, to which they know by experience that draught and its inseparable companions, rinderpest and famine, may at any time put an end. The uncertain nature of their condition developed among the Maasai a sense of precaution, a worry for the

---

[63] P.H. Gulliver, *art. cit.* (1969) 234-241.

future.[64] Cattle constitutes the only capital of the Maasai, the only assurance for the future. He knows it to be vulnerable, precarious, exposed to the hazards of climatological variations and to the arbitrariness of epizootics. Hence the absolute priority which he accords to the concern of incessantly and at all costs increasing its numerical potential. His great and constant preoccupation is that of constituting a flock which is as numerous as possible. The more heads of cattle there are, the more chance there is to have some survive in times of adversity.

Gulliver relates Maasai conservatism to these ecological givens. He holds that for a people living in such conditions, the exterior world in terms of African farmers and, later, of the various representatives of the European world had little to offer which was of direct use or which represented an immediate advantage for them. If it was relatively easy for the administration to see what could be done for the development of a population of sedentarized agriculturalists living in regions which were favorable to the human being, it was much less easy for it to propose to the pastoralists of East Africa innovations the use for which could not immediately be perceived by the participants. The severe limitations of the physical environment of the Maasai do not particularly invite experimentation and do not stimulate adventure. In the eyes of the inhabitants, change is affected with the sign of potential disaster. To distance oneself from the paved ways of the experience of the past comes down psychologically to compromise and mortgage the future. An agriculturist can more easily allow himself the luxury of experimenting with new crops and methods. He has the leisure of launching

---

[64] One usually denies African societies this mid-term perspective on the future. D. Zahan, *Religion, spiritualité et pensée africaines* (Paris, 1970) 141: "Alors qu'il existe des termes variés pour marquer les différentes étapes du passé, depuis l'hier' jusqu'à l' 'autrefois', il est assez frappant de constater que dans beaucoup de langues africaines l'avenir se trouve peu différencié. C'est surtout en fonction d'un avenir très proche, le 'demain' qu'il est caractérisé abstraitement." J. Mbiti, *African Religions and Philosophy* (London, 1969) 22: "Beyond a few months from now, the African concept of time is silent and indifferent. This means that the future is virtually non-existent as *actual* time, apart from the relatively short projection of the present up to two years hence." Cfr. J. Mbiti, *New Testament Eschatology in an African Background* (London, 1971) 24. A. Kagame, "Aperception empirique du temps et conception de l'histoire dans la pensée bantu," in P. Ricœur et al., *Les cultures et le temps* (Paris, 1975) 117: "Etant donné que la culture bantu limite à l'année la sériation du temps, on peut penser qu'un individu ne peut former des plans allant au delà de ce laps de temps divisé en douze mois." For a pertinent criticism of this 'classical' view, see W. De Mahieu, "Le temps dans la culture komo," *Africa. Journal of the International African Institute* (1973) 13-15; J. Ayoade, "Time in Yoruba Thought," in R. Wright (ed.), *African Philosophy: An Introduction* (Washington, 1977); L. Bouffard, "La perspective future chez les Africains," *Revue d'Ethnopsychologie* (1982); Kwame Gyekye, *An Essay on African Philosophical Thought. The Akan Conceptual Scheme* (Cambridge, 1987) 169-177.

himself into change while limiting in advance the risks. He can take care to assure himself of at least his subsistence by effecting innovative experiences on one part of the land, using the rest to cultivate traditional plants according to tested methods. For the herdsman, the margin of security which would permit him to launch himself into novelties is much narrower. If they would fail, the experimentations with innovations would risk exposing the flocks to mortal danger. The administration has never ceased to advise the Maasai to limit the volume of their flocks so as to reduce pressure on available grazing grounds which over-grazing threatened with degradation and even desertification. This advice was of course in vain, because it was irreconcilable with the essential purpose of all Maasai who desire precisely to constantly increase the number of their cattle so as to be assured of a livelihood in case meager years would announce themselves – and experience proves that they will inexorably come! European experts in breeding also invited the Maasai to improve the economic value of their animals by taking appropriate measures so that they produce more milk and more meat. But the Maasai asked themselves: who will tell whether such animals won't be less resistant to draught and famine than those which we have been breeding in the past? They have judged that it would be more prudent not to run the risk of carrying the eventual costs of the experience. The efforts to convince the Maasai of the necessity of sedentarization also failed. In their eyes, sedentarization threatened the possibilities for mobility and weakened their flexibility, both of which are so essential in times of draught and famine. And we could continue to enumerate examples. Finally, Gulliver points out that in general the new perspectives which the European culture offered to the Maasai must have seemed rather unattractive in terms of their traditional socio-cultural system.

One must be careful not to confuse the theory of Gulliver with that of R.S. Merrill. In introducing the ecological element, Gulliver effectively advances an answer to the question of why the Maasai reacted in a way so different from that of other ethnic groups to pressure from the administration to change. Recent studies on social change among the Kamba during the colonial period seem at first sight to confirm the ecological hypothesis. Analyzing the response of the Kamba to the agricultural and commercial innovations in Machakos district, J.F. Munro remarks that this turns out to be different in the Northern and in the Western parts, on the one hand, and in the Southern and the Eastern regions, on the other hand. The spontaneous initiatives of engaging in the new areas of the economy are many in the first and rare or non-existent in the second. We are thus dealing with the same ethnic group situated within the borders of the same district and within the same population adhering to a common culture, but with different responses to social change. Hence, it seems that the respective reactions are linked to ecological variations. From the ecological point of view, Machakos district presents itself as an intermediary and transitory zone between the Kikuyu country, characterized by a high agricultural potential, on the one hand, and the Maasai reserve, where the climatological and ecological conditions in general favor the pastoral life, on the other. The variations in the reaction to the innovations coincide with variations in the ecological environment. It is in those regions neighboring the land of the Kikuyu that a positive response is registered, while in the zones related from the ecological point of view to the Maasai reserve, the call to change remains almost without response.[65] The work of M. O'Leary on the Kamba inhabiting Kitui district corroborates these views.[66]

We do not pretend that the economic marginality of the Maasai herdsmen had no influence on their attitude and comportment. Nevertheless, the thesis of Gulliver does not completely satisfy us. It is not entirely free of the tautological touch which we discerned above. This is manifested especially in the last part of the discussion which, at closer look, resembles a simple reaffirmation of the phenomenon sought to be explained rather than a real explanation. What Gulliver says concerning the lack of interest manifested from the perspective of the traditional socio-cultural system of the Maasai with respect to the innovations of foreign origin could be applied with as much justice to the traditional system of many other African peoples, agricultural peoples included. It is precisely a question of knowing why these other peoples have chosen to adapt – that is to simultaneously search for a way to insert themselves in the new world and for a way of inserting the innovations of the latter into their own traditional system – while the Maasai, in keeping a distance, have taken the opposite option. Taking everything into consideration, it seems difficult to sustain the view that the ecological factor really provides an answer to this question. We must remember here that before the famous treaties of 1904 and 1911, the majority of the Maasai lived in regions which lent themselves remarkably well to the practice of agriculture, which made them desirable to white colonists. Moreover, certain Maasai groups still today occupy certain ecological niches which are anything but poor and marginalized, and where agriculture is perfectly possible. In fact, no less than sixty percent of the territories presently occupied by the Maasai of Kenya enter into this category.[67] That is why they presently arouse the interest of Kenyan

---

[65] J.F. Munro, *Colonial Rule and the Kamba. Social Change in the Kenya Highlands 1889-1939* (Oxford, 1975) 185.

[66] M. O'Leary, *The Kitui Akamba. Economic and Social Change in Semi-Arid Kenya* (Nairobi, 1984.)

[67] Kenya Rangelands Environment Monitoring Unit, *Population Stocking Rates and Distribution of Wildlife and Livestock on the Mara and Loita Plains* (Nairobi, 1980.)

and Tanzanian agriculturalists. Like the district of Machakos, the Maasai reserve is not ecologically homogenous. Hence, it is highly significant that, contrary to what happens among the Kamba, this diversification of the environment does not give way to different responses to the external stimuli of social change. It is thus not a matter of speaking of ecological constraints. In other words, the Maasai were not in the past nor are they in the present inexorably forced to embrace the pastoral life which is theirs. The agricultural option was in the past open to all and, to some, still is. Moreover, agriculture is not the only possible alternative. Many other Africans have chosen to be migrant workers, proletarians, merchants, artisans or petty bourgeois. All these options were not in the past and are still not prohibited to the Maasai because of their traditional lifestyle. To pretend the contrary is to feed into a simplistic and naive ecological determinism.[68]

---

[68] With regard to the influence of the natural environment upon culture, contemporary anthropology attempts to avoid the excesses of both determinism and possibilism. Cfr. J. Barreau, "Ecologie," in R. Creswell (ed.), *Eléments d'ethnologie. Vol. II* (Paris, 1975); M. Sahlins, *Culture and Practical Reason* (Chicago, 1976.) For a critique of an excessive ecological orientation in the study of pastoral societies, particularly in those of East Africa, see M. Godelier, *Horizons, trajets marxistes en anthropologie* (Paris, 1973) 47; G. Dahl - A. Hjort, *Having Herds. Pastoral Herd Growth and Household Economy* (Stockholm, 1976); G. Dahl, *Suffering Grass. Subsistence and Society of Waso Borana* (Stockholm, 1979) 11-12.

THE DYNAMICS OF SOCIAL RELATIONS

R.L. Tignor tackles the problem of Maasai resistance in a more nuanced way.[69] According to him, the decisive explanatory element is to be sought in the dynamics of social relations, more particularly in the role played by the warriors or *ilmurran*.[70] He states that the most elaborate system of age classes in East Africa is that of the Maasai.[71] Nowhere in the region does it have such a profound influence and exercise such a determinative function for the system of government as with the Nilotic pastoralists of Kenya and Tanzania. Almost no political power, no system of authority counterbalances the impact of the age classes. Theoretically, it is the members of the class of elders who possess the supreme political power in the system. Nevertheless, in practice the warriors remain capable of independent initiative. In fact the functioning of the system relies on a fragile equilibrium between elders and warriors. If the final decision in important tribal affairs belongs to the former, the latter enjoy a certain degree of political autonomy and prerogatives sufficient to resolve their own specific problems. Moreover, it has happened that the *ilmurran* turned against an elder or a group of elders who appeared to them as particularly oppressive, by organizing a cattle raid or a punitive expedition against them. At the end of the nineteenth and the beginning of the twentieth century, the Maasai passed through a series of natural disasters and military trials,[72] of which one of the

---

[69] R.L. Tignor, *art. cit.* (1972); *op. cit.* (1976) 73-93.

[70] Singular: *olmurrani*, plural: *ilmurran*.

[71] This affirmation seems wrong to me. The *gada* age class system of the Oromo, particularly as practised by the Borana, is infinitely more complex than that of the Maasai. See A. Legesse, *Gada. Three Approaches to the Study of African Society* (New York - London, 1973) 50, which rightly describes the system of the Borana as "an extreme development of a type of social structure known to anthropologists as age-sets" and as "an institution that appears so exaggerated that it is readily dismissed by laymen and scholars alike as a sociological anomaly." Cfr. P. Baxter, "Boran Age-Sets and Generation-Sets - Gada: a Puzzle or a Maze?," in P. Baxter - U. Almagor (eds.), *Age, Generation and Time. Some Features of East African Age Organization* (London, 1978.)

[72] Cfr. V. Neckebrouck, *op. cit.* (1978) 53.

consequences was the development, especially among the warriors, of the phenomenon of anomy.[73] One of the aspects accompanying the agitation and the perturbations which characterized this period is the accentuation of the tendency of the warriors to affirm their independence with regard to the elders. The Maasai informants explicitly point to this evolution of social relations in the tribe. The establishment of a colonial regime was not of the nature of facilitating a return to ancient equilibrium. It carried with it, on the contrary, a number of new problems and launched new challenges. Among these, it is without question the massive displacements organized by the treaties of 1904 and 1911 which created the most explosive situations. But to the surprise of contemporary observers, the forced double exodus took place without notable resistance by the Maasai. This was due essentially to the persuasive power of Lenana, at that time the main ritual expert of the tribe, and of the most influential elders who ended up by successfully convincing the people, and the warriors in particular, that all armed resistance was totally useless and could only attract new and even worse misfortunes upon the tribe. This abstention from violence was not without importance for the future of the people. It meant that the Maasai transferred their traditional institutions, and in particular their warrior organization, almost intact to their new environment, the colonizer not having felt the need to destroy them. In view of the role which will be assigned to the warrior class in the subsequent history of the tribe, the absence of decisive military confrontation between the Maasai and the colonizer carries after all a certain importance in as far as such a settling of affairs through arms would have certainly brought about the dismantling of the military organization of the defeated. But, as one can see, the significance of the avoidance of armed conflict is founded here in a manner other than that of Sandford and Mungeam.

In studying the activities, the intentions and the testimonies of certain members of the colonial administration in the Maasai districts, Tignor shows in a concrete and convincing way that the people have not been deprived of initiatives by the administration deliberately aimed at its transformation and its modernization. All theses which take as the point of departure and the corner stone for their argument the theme of isolation find themselves hereby debilitated. The author also has the merit of searching for an explanation of their conservatism from the Maasai themselves, thus putting into application the above mentioned principle which considers the attitude toward modernization to be the result of

---

[73] This evolution is in every aspect comparable to that which, according to us, has taken place in the same epoch among the sets of Kikuyu warriors, more especially among the Kikuyu who formed the pioneering fringe of the people at the borders of the tribal territory. *Ibidem*, p. 113-114.

an interaction between the activity of the colonizer and the response of the colonized. What are the results he reaches? In any case, not that of a static, vague and almost mystical psychological constellation, that of an unchangeable mentality in which some root the Maasai conservatism. Rather, he directs our attention to the social structure, in particular toward the opposition between elders and warriors. After the famous Maasai treaties, when all the members of the tribe found themselves entirely concentrated in a single reserve to the south of the railway linking Mombasa to the capital of Uganda, the warriors engaged themselves three times in an attempt at armed revolt against the British. This was successively in 1918, 1922 and 1935. In all three cases, the *ilmurran* acted not only in independence from the elders, but against their advice and will. In the three cases also, the revolt was caused by attempts at modernization effected by the government and directed against them.

In 1918, the rebellion exploded on the occasion of the forced recruitment of schoolchildren so as to populate the new government school established in Narok. Moreover, as district officer Bell later relates concerning this event, the recruitment of the schoolchildren had always constituted one of the grievances most profoundly felt by the Maasai. Tignor shows that this independent action of the warriors probably slowed down the efforts toward scholarization in the reserve. From this moment forth, district commissioner Hemstedt, who was the architect and the advocate of educational policy among the Maasai, considered the organization of the *ilmurran* to be the basis and source of Maasai conservatism. Thus, during the following two decades, the administration made an effort to identify and suppress those aspects of the warrior organization which seemed to block social change. Of course the government had supplementary reasons to oppose the warrior system. Because of the continuing raids which they organized, often without the endorsement of the elders, the *ilmurran* constituted a permanent threat to law and order. But the attacks of the administration against their organization not only aimed at facilitating the recruitment of schoolchildren and at putting an end to *raiding*. They were an integral part of a larger program, destined to reestablish the traditional functioning of the political order where the supreme authority ideally lay with the elders. Why did the government pursue this latter goal? Precisely, says the author, because the elders showed themselves to be more disposed to collaborate with the government in its efforts to modernize Maasai society. Hemstedt wanted the Maasai to entrust their children to the schools, to practice agriculture, to lower the size of their flocks by selling more cattle to the merchants, to collaborate in the establishment of a milk industry and in the construction of a road system, and to orient themselves more toward money economy and modern models of consumption. The favorable disposition of the elders toward this reformist program of the government is not difficult to understand. Not only did the constant lack of discipline of the *ilmurran* represent a permanent challenge to their authority, it also made them suffer economic losses. The independent razzias of the warriors drew serious sanctions in the form of monetary fines or confiscation of cattle which, imposed upon the whole of the local community, hit without discrimination *ilmurran* and elders. The defense of their political status along with their economic interests thus instilled in the elders an attitude of collaboration. As well, perhaps they were less than ignorant of the fact that among their Kikuyu neighbors, this attitude allowed the 'chiefs' to enrich themselves rapidly.

Whatever the case, the attempts by the administration at manipulation of the initiation system, in view of reducing the length of time during which the young traditionally served as warriors, provoked a new attempt at armed resistance on the part of the *ilmurran* in 1922. The third rebellion took place in 1935, under the administration of Major Buxton. Like his predecessor Hemstedt, Buxton was convinced of the need to completely transform the Maasai society for it to enter the modern world. And he, too, felt certain that the *ilmurran* constituted the key to the problem of tribal conservatism. Moreover, from the beginning of his nomination as district commissioner of Narok, he affirmed that he would continue to lead a policy of suppression of the warrior age classes. He took charge over the district at a time when Kenya passed through an economic depression. As this coincided with a period of draught, the Maasai economy found itself seriously affected and the people underwent great difficulties to pay their taxes. On the one hand, this situation limited the possibilities for action of the district commissioner. But on the other hand it seemed to facilitate the execution of some of his plans. The *ilmurran* would construct a road which led from Narok to Mau, their work discharging them from taxes. The construction of roads constitutes an important factor in modernization. It opens entire regions to economic contacts and familiarizes the population with new techniques and work disciplines.[74] The elders and even the spokesmen of the *ilmurran*[75] promised their collaboration. But the work had hardly started when the warriors protested and refused to continue the task. A brief confrontation with the forces of order ensued, followed by the flight of all the workers. Thus another effort toward modernization ended prematurely.

---

[74] On this subject, we refer to A. B. Hellbom, "Sociocultural Changes Resulting from Road Construction in Areas of Difficult Access," in B. Berdichewsky, (ed.), *Anthropology and Social Change in Rural Areas* (Den Haag - Paris - New York, 1979.)

[75] These *ilaiguenak* were different from the military leaders of the warriors.

Tignor advances a more nuanced and more diversified reaction to moderniz-ation than all the other authors which we have thusfar reviewed. He acknowl-edges that the meaning of social change was not apprehended in the same way by all sections of the population. In particular, it carried a different meaning for the elders than for the warriors. Traditionally, the relations between these two groups were charged with considerable potential for conflict. The disrupting elements of the end of the previous century and tensions resulting from the coming of colonial domination came to accentuate this aspect of the social structure. The warrior state constitutes an essentially transitory phase in the life-cycle. The *ilmurran* were supposed to use this period of their career to the maximum in order to constitute the initial core of the flock which they were destined to form later, when custom would force them to abandon the warrior activities and to focus on the development of a home, the basis of their economic subsistence and the sign of their material security, of their social prestige and their political influence. One of the most popular ways to gather cattle in a short time was the practice of *raiding*. Hence, every effort on the part of the adminis-tration and the elders to stop or limit this activity, which was traditionally held in high esteem, was not only felt to contradict custom, but also considered an attempt to refuse the *ilmurran* the possibility of assuring their future economic well-being. Similarly, the decision to shorten the period of the warrior state could only be interpreted by the concerned *ilmurran* as an attack against the social and economic status of the warriors. Indeed, they would have less time than before to give themselves over to the practice of *raiding* which was reserved for the warriors. All of these restrictions had as a result that at the end of their 'military service' many *ilmurran* were no longer wealthy enough to get married. In these circumstances, they were left with no other alternative than to go and live with their fathers and brothers and work for them. This dependence lowered their status and was highly dreaded by the young Maasai. Traditionally, it was the *ilmurran* who enjoyed the highest prestige in Maasai society. In the eyes of the Maasai, the years as warrior represent the happiest time and the zenith of their life. To leave the stage of *olmurrani* for that of elder was for many Maasai an agonizing experience and the pain which accompanies it is symbolically inscribed in the rite of passage consecrating the event. Hence, the colonial order tended to completely deprive the *olmurrani* of the privileges of his status and of the prestige which surrounded it. The *Pax Britannica* rendered the function of defense of the community superfluous, and the organization of razzias was forbidden: in the new order, the *olmurrani* no longer has any function and the formerly admired and feared hero now finds himself lowered to the level of a socially useless and cumbersome unemployed who is threatened with an uncertain future.[76] All this while the elders were able to benefit from the colonial situation and to reach respectable positions within the framework of the new administration.

The research of Tignor, essentially well-documented, constitutes an interesting contribution to the study of the origins of Maasai conservatism. Nevertheless, a series of questions remain unresolved. It is an excellent principle not to look at the tribe as a monolithic entity and instead to take account of the coexistence within its contours of different groups which are themselves composed of different individuals who may react in diverse ways to the opportunities and to the constraints of the colonial situation, to the dangers and to the possibilities inherent in social changes and in the perspective of modernization. Nevertheless, this does not allow us to lose sight of the fact that the case which occupies us places us in the presence of a people of which not only a particular section, but in a sense the population as a whole has, with remarkable continuity, constancy and obstinacy kept itself at a distance from Western influence for a full century. The analysis of Tignor explains very well the motives of resistance of the *ilmurran* for the period between the two World Wars. But is this sufficient to account for the conservatism of the entire Maasai society during the whole colonial period and beyond? For if it is plausible that the elders would have been able to profit from the colonial juncture, that is to enrich themselves and increase their authority, in reality the Maasai society did not produce the collaborator chiefs so characteristic of the colonial regime of the neighboring acephalous society of the Kikuyu. There is still another enigma. If the position of the elder opened such possibilities of economic, social, and political promotion to those who held it, why did the *ilmurran*, rather than applaud a measure which would allow them to reach this privileged status more rapidly than foreseen by the tradition, on the contrary oppose it?[77] The losses suffered following the reduction of the military service would, if the thesis of the author is correct, easily be caught up and compensated by the fruits of the collaboration. Finally, the author forgets a fact, which was nevertheless noted since the nineteenth century, namely that the elders profited just as much from the razzias carried out by the *ilmurran* as did the *ilmurran* themselves. Not only were they in charge of the captured animals until their sons were old enough to marry, but a part of the

---

[76] While in the field, I have heard more than enough such complaints. The grievance was registered at least since 1919. See G. Sandford, *op. cit.*, p. 5.

[77] We allude to the armed conflict of 1922, to which we referred earlier, and which was provoked by the attempt of the administration to shorten the length of the military service (the state of *olmurrani*) and thereby bring nearer the moment of promotion to the status of elder.

40

booty was given to them for good.[78] The economic interests of the one and the other were thus not as opposed as we are led to believe.

The author seems to have foreseen at least the first two of our objections. He did in fact take care to note that the three attempts at revolt effected by the *ilmurran* had a double consequence, capable, according to him, of adequately explaining the general – almost universal – character of the conservative choice as well as the constancy of the people in guarding this option. On the one hand, the most significant effect of the rebellions was a renewed weakening of the influence of the elders, and a consequent extension of that of the conservative warriors. On the other hand, the violent rebellion persuaded the British, who by now had come to hate armed confrontations[79], of the need to slow the rhythm of the modernization of the Maasai. Because our third question is not addressed by the author, the answer implied by the two others is far from totally convincing. The reduction of the prestige and the authority of the elders, the fact that they lacked a basis of power in society does not suffice to explain why colonial chiefs who were really collaborators did not emerge among the Maasai. They were, according to Tignor, unable to create their own para-administrative and military organization, which are indispensable for whoever seeks to maintain himself in power and, among other things, to force the move to a highly unpopular social change. One may indeed admit that it must have been somewhat easier for the Kikuyu chiefs, however detested by the population, to assure themselves of a certain support thanks to the kinship institutions and to the territorial units which counterbalanced more than was the case with the Maasai the impact of the age class organization and the feeling of absolute loyalty generated by it.

But another objection arises. The attempts at revolt upon which the author bases himself happen to be the exclusive work of the *ilmurran* of only one section of the Maasai, the Purko. These have tried in vain to drag the warriors of the other sections along the way of violent resistance. But in spite of the fact that the *ilmurran* could everywhere assent to the same grievances, the Purko warriors did not succeed in convincing their confreres to follow them. These remained ultimately submissive to the elders who advised them to abstain from violent actions. This important fact is known by the author. But he fails to stop

---

[78] G.A. Fischer, *Das Maasailand* (Hamburg, 1885); J. Thomson, *Through Masai Land. A Journey of Exploration among Snowclad Volcanic Mountains and Strange Tribes of Eastern Equatorial Africa* (London, 1885.) Cfr. H.A. Fosbrooke, "The Maasai Age-Group System as a Guide to Tribal Chronology," *African Studies* (1956.)

[79] Because of the turbulences which they provoked in certain political circles and in public opinion in the United Kingdom.

and face the question which it generates. Why did the elders not take advantage of the loyalty of the *ilmurran* to make them swallow the politics of social change of which, according to the author, the elders would have been the propagators because they were also its beneficiaries? The basis of power was not lacking in these cases. Once again, the limits of the validity of the analysis of the author become clear. Strictly speaking, the justifying materials advanced do not support the plausibility of the explanation except for a well determined period, i.e. the epoch between the two wars, and even then only for a particular section of the Maasai. The point of departure for the author's argumentation, in itself very valuable, according to which it is important to distinguish in the population constituting a tribe different layers which, confronted with the perspective of modernization, each have their particular motives and their own way of reacting, ends by turning against him. If one assents to the introduction of a distinction between elders and warriors, there is no reason to surrender this spirit of nuances when it forces us to question our conclusions. If it is good to be aware of the non-congruence between the attitude of the elders and those of the *ilmurran*, it is equally recommended to remain attentive to the cleavage separating the behavior of the Purko *ilmurran* from that of the warriors of the other sections.

It seems to us that the corrective which must be brought to the thesis of Tignor is to pretend that, if it is true that there has been a conflict between the elders and the Purko *ilmurran* concerning modernization, it hardly bore upon the ground of the question, but only upon the method and the tactics adopted in order to survive and not be crushed by a colonizer perceived as malevolent and hostile. For the elders, the core of the conflict was never the abandonment or the continuity of their pastoral life, nor even the legitimacy and value of the class of the *ilmurran*. Their loyalty toward both was never doubted. The issue was control over the warriors. This preoccupation is not new. On the contrary, it constitutes an aspect familiar to traditional life. Such presentation of the facts harmonizes with the reality of Maasai conservatism as characteristic of a people in its totality, as well as with the idea of a certain differentiation in the reaction to foreign intrusion. The fundamental attitude of the tribe, common to the elders and to the warriors, is one of rejection of change and modernization. The very study of Tignor carries evidence in favor of this thesis. Discussing the incident of 1918 concerning the recruitment of schoolchildren, he writes: "To be sure, the elders resented the taking of their children, but again counselled the futility of resistance."[80] In the light of these facts, the weight of the divergence of opinion between the elders and the warriors appears to be much less important

---

[80] R.L. Tignor, *art. cit.* (1972) 282.

than that which the author would make us believe. Because, as we have pointed out above, the former have in fact not exploited – even in circumstances in which they would have been able to benefit by it – the economic advantages offered by the colonization which, according to Tignor, would account for the opposite options of the two groups, it seems much more preferable to understand these in terms of difference of temperament, of style and of method which have since of old characterized the approach and behavior of the members of the respective groups. Here too, the study of Tignor offers certain elements sustaining this interpretation. The author dedicates a few lines to the career of a certain Ole Gelishu who, after having been as *olmurrani* a zealous leader of the armed resistance, once become an elder, set himself to subdue the violence of the warriors, to reduce their independence, and to assist the government in its efforts to reduce the period spent as *olmurrani*. Tignor observes that this spectacular reversal does not exclude for Gelishu a profound continuity of thought and intention. Years of experience had not only convinced Gelishu of the vanity and the absurdity of armed resistance. He also came to understand that the anomy and the turbulence of the warriors did nothing but bring upon the people the dissatisfaction of the government which, in turn, doubled the pressures on the tribe so as to force it into the way of social change. But Gelishu wanted precisely to prevent such an evolution. And the best strategy to do this seemed to him to consist in making small concessions in the hope of being able to remain fundamentally conservative in essential matters. The ultimate purpose of Gelishu thus remained constant. The *olmurrani* and the *olpayian* [elder] which succeeded one another were inspired by the same aversion toward innovation and were animated by an identical zeal for the preservation of the authentic Maasai pastoral tradition. Only the style, the method and the strategy had changed. The exuberance, the aggressiveness, and the martial language of the *olmurrani* had given way to the wisdom, moderation, prudence and sense of responsibility of the elder. In the image of that between Gelishu the *olmurrani* and Gelishu the *olpayian*, the conflict between warriors and elders is not an opposition between collaboration and resistance, but between two different ways of safeguarding fidelity to the pastoral vocation. It does not touch the ground of the attitude to be adopted toward modernization, but concerns the most adequate way of resisting it without paying for that resistance with the destruction of the people.

In formulating these critical remarks and this alternative reading in 1978, I did not know that they would be confirmed in a convincing way the following year by the thorough historical study of J.L. Berntsen.[81] Since then, my field-

---

[81] J.L. Berntsen, *op. cit.*, p. 310-312.

work on the Maasai has considerably reinforced my reticence with regard to the thesis of Tignor. It appeared more clearly to me that the conflict between elders and warriors is part and parcel of the very structure of Maasai society. This society develops and functions by means of a series of structural oppositions, of which that existing between the *ilmurran* and the *ilpayiani* is only one.[82] Hence, the deep reason for it cannot be based on considerations derived from something which in the Maasai history was experienced merely as a contingent event: the encounter with the colonial regime. Similarly, the phenomenon of conflict cannot be reduced to its purely economical aspects. It encompasses other dimensions. Several cultural traits and symbolic aspects accompanying the foundation of the *manyata*[83] and certain characteristics of the life which the warriors lead there, but upon which we cannot elaborate here, allow consideration of the opposition between the two groups as a projection on the collective plane of the conflictual relation between father and son in which the problem of succession probably constitutes the central core and the essential catalyst.[84] But that is not everything. Up to a certain point, the warriors and the elders adhere to entirely different conceptions of society and hence to conceptions of social ethics which are diametrically opposed. The impact of these radically divergent conceptions plays a role in the structuration of social oppositions. The elders, chiefs of their respective families and responsible for their well-being, represent the individualism, particularism, and authoritarianism of the patrilineage. They incarnate the hierarchical principle and the ethics of the private or family property of certain means of production (cattle), of competition, of differentiation, and of the vertical structuration of society. On the other hand, the organization of life in the *manyata* aspires to the establishment of a regime and a way of life which tends toward abolishing precisely everything which the society of the elders pursues and defends. The *ilmurran* seek to establish a universalist, interdependent, and egalitarian morality. They attempt to organize society according to the principles of homogeneity and horizontality, to abolish every trace of individualism, particularism, authoritarianism, competition and private property.

---

[82] In the context of the present essay it is impossible to develop and illustrate this point. It would involve elaborating a whole monograph of Maasai society and culture.

[83] Camp where the *ilmurran* normally reside. The term possesses other meanings which are of no relevance to us here.

[84] It is not surprising that P. Spencer, *The Samburu. A Study of Gerontocracy in a Nomadic Tribe* (London, 1965) 100-101, and P. Spencer, *The Maasai of Matapato. A Study of Rituals of Rebellion* (Manchester - London, 1988) 271-274, interprets these aspects in the light of Freudian and Frazerian theories. On the universal relevance of the problem of succession, see J.H. Vaughan, "A Reconsideration of Divine Kingship," in I. Karp - C.S. Bird (eds.), *Explorations in African Systems of Thought* (Bloomington, 1980.)

It does not seem exaggerated to affirm that the *ilmurran* seek to permanently establish that state of *communitas* so well described by V. Turner.[85]

The rituals which go together with the erection of the warrior camp take the bearing of a real assault of the familial and patriarchal system. The warrior leaves the paternal domain and, at this occasion, tears away the mother from her husband and leads her to the *manyata* where she lives until her son is himself an elder. His uncircumcised brothers and sisters also accompany him. A part of the cattle of the father is equally confiscated. These uprootings take place in the context of a razzia in true and proper form against the paternal domain. The life of the *olmurrani* thus as a rule begins with an attack against the institution of the patriarchal family toward which the *olmurrani* behaves as an instance of disintegration. The razzia held at this occasion spontaneously evokes the idea of the rituals of rebellion once described by M. Gluckman.[86] This is except for a few differences which have been well underlined by P. Spencer. The raid against the paternal domain is not the expression of a passing protest, symbolically translating a social conflict and followed by a return to normal life. In fact, the sons do not return to the paternal hearth. As they leave the warrior life, it is normally to become elders and to found their own family. We are moreover in the presence of a clear exception to the rule, stated by Gluckman, according to which the ritual conflict never invades the heart of the elementary family because that would put the most fundamental social relations in danger. The particularity of the Maasai ritual consists precisely in penetrating the very heart of the family institution.[87] Once established in the *manyata*, the *olmurrani* continues to be submitted constantly to the constraints imposed by an ideology which seeks to belittle the ties of family and clan in favor of solidarity between members of the *olporror* (age class) which transcends kinship relations and the territorial community. The members of the *olporror* are bound to behave friendly towards one another at all times and in all circumstances. Private property is in principle taboo. Everything must be shared.[88] They live together and freely cooperate regardless of their lineage, clan, or territorial affiliation. The habitations where they are forbidden to tread during the night are precisely those of the warriors belonging to their own clan. They are not allowed to drink the milk of

---

[85] V. Turner, *The Ritual Process. Structure and Anti-Structure* (Harmondsworth, 1974.)

[86] M. Gluckman, *Custom and Conflict in Africa* (Oxford, 1956); M. Gluckman, *Politics, Law and Ritual in Tribal Society* (Oxford, 1965.)

[87] P. Spencer, *op. cit.* (1988) 271.

[88] In the contemporary context, this extends till the most prestigious possessions: radios, watches, bicycles, etc.

cows which belong to their family or to their clan. They are bound to respect other nutrition taboos: only milk and meat can be consumed; the meat which they eat cannot be seen by a married woman; they may consume milk only in the presence of a member of the *olporror*; in drinking this liquid, they will watch out that certain parts of their body (arms, legs, shoulders) touch in order to underline that nothing may be put between them which could separate them. These measures contribute to pushing the warrior to avoid the paternal domain and to look for the company of members of his own age class. As such he liberates himself more and more from family bonds and progressively internalizes the ethics of solidarity, equality and universality which characterizes the warriors and which is so opposed to that which reigns in the family kraal. To this may be added that the fifteen years passed as a warrior are considered by the Maasai to be the apogee of their life. It is the time of the razzias of cattle, of the raids against enemy sections or neighboring people, the glorious time of the *res gestae*. The morality which reigns at this time of their life participates in the aura of perfection which surrounds it. Once he acquires the status of elder, the Maasai changes his life and morality.[89] The corporate life eminently active in the heart of the age class practically terminates in a rather brutal way. It is true that the *olporror* continues to exist, but in practice the involvement of the *olpayian* in its activities and ceremonies is very limited. The elders consider themselves, and are considered by others, as having finished their public and active life. They stay at home and take care of their wives, their children and their flocks. Their preoccupations and their worries are henceforth mainly linked to this reduced world and in these circumstances, it is not surprising that their ethics tend to become more particularistic, individualistic, localized, and attentive to the interests of their person, their family and the local community.[90] Of course it would be necessary to make several nuances in this reading of the Maasai society which is strongly marked by contrasting traits; to show, for example, that in practice, fragments of *communitas* survive in the society of elders, while elements of particularism come to 'corrupt' the society of the *ilmurran*. This does not preclude that at the level of the description which the Maasai themselves provide

---

[89] The passage from one state to the other often goes with a psychological crisis and with a state of depression.

[90] My interpretation of Maasai society is largely corroborated by the recent study of P. Spencer, *op. cit.*, 1988. See especially pp. 226, 250, 267, 274, 276.

of their society[91] the contrast is radical. One will have understood that this double morality does not fall from heaven, but that it derives directly from the coexistence of the two central institutions which form the basis of Maasai social structure. The contradiction on the level of social ethics reflects that which exists between the solidarity with the age class and the loyalty toward the lineage. It will from thenceforth continue to contribute maintaining a conflict between elders and warriors as long as the Maasai judge it necessary to ensure the reproduction of their society simultaneously by means of the patriarchal lineage and the system of age classes, or more precisely, of the *enkang* or patriarchal domain and of the *manyata*. Indeed, the simple conjugation of family structure and system of age classes does not automatically engender an opposition on the level of ethical ideology. In certain neighboring Bantu societies, for example that of the Kikuyu, the two institutions coexist without clear marks of the ethical dichotomy characteristic of the ideology of the Nilotic pastoralists. It is the specific way in which the warrior phase of the male curriculum is organized among the latter, in particular their alienation from the *enkang* and their prolonged regrouping in the *manyata*, as well as the ideology which expresses this spatial structuration, which are pertinent for an understanding of Maasai situation and behavior.

---

[91] I must specify that my presentation of the ethics, or more precisely of the opposed ethical tendencies is principally, though not exclusively, based on the discourse of the *ilmurran*. For obvious reasons, the elders are much more unwilling to discuss the basis and motivations of their social behavior.

ETHICS

We deliberately dwelled at some length on the ideological dimension of the conflict between elders and warriors. In his explanation of the attitude of the Maasai toward Christianity, P. Rigby[92] indeed makes a strong case for the ideology of the pastoralists, particularly for their social ethics. The position of the author can be briefly summarized as follows. The conditions of the reproduction of pastoral society demand and effectively generate a specific ideology, different from the ideological formations produced by agricultural societies. Pastoral society could not survive without a moral code characterized by renunciation to the right of the personal appropriation of some of the essential economical resources such as land, grazing grounds, water ponds and salt deposits. Simultaneously, such a society demands a spirit of solidarity, mutual sharing, and of active and friendly cooperation. Finally, it commands the abandonment of every relationship of exploitation of the other, as well as the creation of solid egalitarian convictions. Indeed, the Maasai ideology entails all of these components. Ideology and mode of production are thus perfectly adjusted. On the level of social structure, it is the system of the age classes which assures the necessary conditions for the reproduction of the community, its mode of production and its ideological exigencies. This explains the subordination of the system of descent and kinship to the organization of age classes with the Maasai, as opposed to the majority of agrarian or agro-pastoral societies where the former type of structure dominates. There is in fact a correlation between the relative domination of one or the other of these principles of organization and the relative importance given either to pastoral or to agricultural activities.

The encounter of the Maasai with the European colonizer must be seen in terms of a confrontation between an egalitarian ideology radically opposed to the appropriation of land, based on collaboration and solidarity, on the one hand,

---

[92] P. Rigby, *op. cit.*, p. 92-122. See also P. Rigby, "Les retombées théoriques des stratégies de développement pastoral en Afrique Orientale," in J. Galaty - D. Aronson - P.C. Salzman (eds.), *L'avenir des peuples pasteurs* (Ottawa, 1983) 172-180.

and on the other a fundamentally individualistic and capitalistic culture, linked to the essentially unegalitarian notion of the exploitation of the work of the other. The Maasai have rapidly discerned not only the incompatibility of the opposite ethical systems transported by the respective civilizations engaged in contact, but also the impossibility for a pastoral society to reproduce itself in the ideological climate of the culture which the invader tended to impose. This is why they chose to preserve themselves from all contamination by Western culture. The Christianity which penetrated East Africa at the end of the nineteenth and the beginning of the twentieth century was not an abstract entity which one could designate as 'the Christian religion.' It presented itself as a specific religious ideology, intimately linked with the capitalistic mode of production prevalent in the industrialized Europe of the times, that is to say as a form of capitalist and colonial Christian ideology. Neither has this fact escaped the attention of the Maasai. They understood the Christian missions to be fundamentally in complicity with the expropriation of the best lands of the tribe to the benefit of the white colonists, and with the efforts of the colonial government to integrate the people in the exploitative network of the capitalist system.[93] It is in the perception of the link between Christian ideology and governmental policy that the fundamental motive of their rejection of the missionary influence lies. Rigby is conscious of the fact that agricultural peoples have not been completely ignorant of this affinity. But he estimates that, as opposed to what is the case in pastoral societies, the capitalist ethic can penetrate agrarian societies without necessarily radically destroying their capability of reproducing themselves. On this topic, the author refers to the thesis of C. Lefebure who affirms: "Because the discourse of members of a segmentary lineage society is rooted in kinship relations which are consubstantial with the group, the alteration in the conditions of realisation of the community does not render it obsolete, even though this alteration may necessitate certain modifications."[94] This would account for the different responses of the Maasai pastoralists and the Bantu agriculturalists to the activities of the missions. The author concludes by expressing the opinion that the Maasai would probably have reacted differently to the message of the missionaries if the latter had presented them with a form of Christianity less linked to the ideology of the peripheral capitalism of the hour and more adapted to the ideological conditions of the reproduction of their society. We can see that by this judgement he rejoins the missiological thesis of which we have spoken at the beginning of this article. Nonetheless, with this difference that he provides

---

[93] One notes to what extent this interpretation contradicts the theories of isolation.

[94] C. Lefebure, "The Specificity of Nomadic Pastoral Societies," in C. Lefebure (ed.), *Pastoral Production and Society* (Cambridge - Paris, 1979) 10.

this thesis with an anthropological underpinning which is lacking in the missiological discourse.

The analysis of P. Rigby represents a stimulating contribution to the understanding of the reaction of East African pastoralists in general, and of the Maasai in particular, with regard to Christianity. At the same time, and notwithstanding this, it does not fail to raise a certain number of issues. First, it makes complete abstraction of the tension existing between the two ethical systems in force among the Maasai, based upon the particular structuration of their society. The principles of descent and kinship are not completely obliterated in favor of that of the organization of age classes, and, by their particular requirements, continue to inform the ethical ideology of the people. That is Rigby's weak point. A. Legesse writes:

> Although the West has developed a most elaborate egalitarian philosophy, in practice it does not and cannot live by that philosophy because it lacks effective institutional mechanisms that can set limits upon the magnitude of social and economic inequalities.[95]

Similarly, Maasai society will show itself incapable of honoring its egalitarian philosophy as long as it allows the internal cohabitation of the organization of age classes and an organizational principle which counterbalances it, that of the patriarchal family. The effort of Rigby would certainly have gained credibility if it had paid more attention to this structural duality with its consequences on the ideological level, and if he had explained himself concerning the reasons for which he treats it as if devoid of pertinence. Regarding the correlation between the relative domination, either of the kinship system or of the age class organization, and the relative importance given to agricultural activities or to pastoral activities, I would moreover like to raise the question of whether the predominance of a principle of organization on the structural plane is necessarily reflected without modification on the existential plane. In a study on four East African peoples which all possess a section of herdsmen besides a section of the population given over to agriculture, R.B. Edgerton writes:

> Contrary to our expectations, preferences concerning age-mates did not differ between pastoralists and farmers. Neither when the choice was between friends and age-mates, nor when it was between clansmen and age-mates, was there any consistent pattern of response that distinguished farmers from pastoralists. The prevailing evaluation of age-mates was ambivalent. Mention of age-mates was as much negative as it was positive, and many respondents expressed both negative and positive feelings at the

---

[95] A. Legesse, *op. cit.*, p. 285.

same time. This finding did not support our expectation that age-mates would be more important among pastoralists.[96]

Of course these so-called surprising results do not teach us anything about the Maasai. But they are useful in directing our attention to the eventual distance which could very well exist among these people too, between the structural given such as it is reconstructed and interpreted by anthropology on the one hand and the existential experience on the other. For the subject with which we are concerned this is not without importance.

To this, Rigby might rejoin that a theory of a double morality, rather than emanating from the Maasai society itself or from faithfully reflecting its discourse, constitutes a product of the interpretative framework of the anthropologist. He would be only partly right. For if it is true that the *ilpayian* would not easily admit adherence to the type of ethical thinking that we attribute to them, on the other hand the *ilmurran* unblushingly reproach them for constantly betraying the high ideals of the authentic tradition. These accusations witness well and proper to the perception of a moral duality in the heart of society. From the point of view of the *ilmurran,* the author thus undoubtedly proceeded to an unjustified homogenization of moral thought. From that of the *ilpayiani,* he practices an abstraction at least to the degree that he contents himself with presenting their morality only on the level of ideology, leaving actual practice in the shadows. It is undeniable that the ideology and the symbolic system[97] constitute essential elements of the culture and way of being of a people. But concrete practice is just as much and with the same rights a part of it. The Maasai transgress the most sacred prescriptions, particularly in times of crisis. For example, in the course of history, complete sections have disappeared from the face of the earth or have been severely reduced following battles, usually caused by resistances to the law of universal access to the elementary means of production (grazing grounds, water ponds, salt depositories.)[98] When one observes daily life in the Maasai society, one quickly becomes aware of the fact that the exploitation of the other is not an unknown phenomenon. The examples are many and often disheartening. They can be found not only in the sphere of relationships with affinal relatives, of which the Maasai say literally that they 'eat' them (*ainosa enkapute*). Nor am I referring exclusively to the exploitation of women and sons, two categories of

---

[96] R.B. Edgerton, *The Individual in Cultural Adaptation. A Study of Four East African Peoples* (Berkeley, 1971) 175.

[97] We mention the symbolic system besides the ideology because certain ceremonies of the elders express what is, in effect, a social ideal identical, or close to that of the *ilmurran.*

[98] For examples, see R.D. Waller, *op. cit.* (1978) et J.L. Berntsen, *op. cit.* (1979.)

people who periodically articulate their protests in rituals of rebellion. No, I speak also of that which the rich practice toward the poor. I have been able to establish repeatedly that the existence of an explicit egalitarian ideology has not prevented the emergence of remarkable inequalities within Maasai society, neither in the past nor in the present. Recent studies confirm the presence of strong social inequalities among other nomadic pastoralists, and the characterization of pastoral societies by the egalitarian and communitarian social relations as per Rigby increasingly appears to be a myth. M. Godelier, for example, writes:

> Chacun sait (...) que chez les peuples pasteurs, la coopération dans la production est beaucoup moins nécessaire que chez les agriculteurs, que le bétail, moyen de production dominant, est une richesse mobilisable immédiatement, ou presque, et qui circule dans des formes non marchandes ou marchandes à une vitesse et dans des proportions sans commune mesure avec la terre dans les sociétés agricoles; que l'adoption de formes marchandes d'échange en est d'autant facilitée chez les éleveurs, et que ces conditions permettent également des phénomènes d'accumulation rapide et immense de richesses entre les mains d'individus ou de quelques groupes familiaux et des phénomènes d'inégalité sociale qui se retrouvent chez les agriculteurs lorsque des formes de propriété privée ou féodale ou étatique du sol se sont développées. (...) Dans ces conditions il est naïf et absurde, scientifiquement, de vouloir masquer les faits de compétition et les faits d'échange marchands au sein d'une société d'éleveurs pour maintenir à tout prix l'idée que les rapports sociaux y sont égalitaires et communautaires.[99]

And A.M. Khazanov writes:

> The specific feature of livestock as a quickly accumulated and easily disposable kind of property provided (...) for the rapid development of property and social differentiation in the nomadic community. (...) The dominant socioeconomic relations within nomadic societies are far from egalitarian. On the contrary, the groups exhibit a definite, sometimes very considerable, social stratification.[100]

In his historical study on poverty in Africa, J. Iliffe rejoins these views: "Pastoralists did not live in the egalitarianism often attributed to herdsmen but

---

[99] M. Godelier, *op. cit.*, p. 21.

[100] A.M. Khazanov, "Characteristic Features of Nomadic Communities in the Eurasian Steppes," in W. Weissleider (ed.), *The Nomadic Alternative. Modes and Models of Interaction in the African-Asian Deserts and Steppes* (Den Haag - Paris, 1978) 122-123.

instead provided some of the continent's clearest evidence of poverty."[101] In African pastoral societies, cattle is the index of prosperity and is distributed unequally across the population. It plays a significant role in the process of social stratification. The control exercised on livestock and on the transactions of cattle functions as the most important instrument for the creation of relations of dominance and dependence.[102] All of this is clearly verified among the Maasai. Expulsion of the most miserable from society, arbitrary favoritism of the father toward certain sons, extreme competition between brothers, explicit discourse clearly differentiating the rich from the poor, marginalization of certain subgroups (*ilkunono*, for example), the existence of a category of people qualified as vagabonds and failures, all constitute so many quasi-structural social phenomena often related to the tensions and rivalries generated by competition. An awareness of these facts does not impose itself solely on the anthropologist in the field. It does not escape the attention of the Maasai themselves. As notes P. Spencer, "the unequal distribution of wealth can no longer be concealed, and their society is seen to be unfair."[103] I have become aware of the fact that the Maasai are often embarrassed by the gap existing between their ideology of strict egalitarianism and solidarity and the inequality and individualism which exist in fact. They like to believe as if, in principle, all the Maasai are willing to exchange, lend, or give animals to one another according to the needs which are felt. If this generous doctrine is not always put into practice, it is explained that this is simply because one has not had the opportunity to apply it, because the quest came at a moment at which one was oneself in difficulties, etc.[104] I do not know to what extent one is aware that, when put into practice, inequality only finds itself more accentuated. In fact, the service provided in the name of the equality ethos reinforces the controlling power and social influence of the

---

[101] J. Iliffe, *op. cit.*, p. 65. See also: Talal Assad, "Equality in Nomadic Social Systems? Notes towards the Dissolution of an Anthropological Category," in C. Lefebure (ed.), *op. cit.*; P.C. Salzman, Inequality and Oppression in Nomadic Society, *ibidem*; G. Dahl, Ecology and Equality: The Boran Case, *ibidem*; J.W. Sutter, Cattle and Inequality: Herd Size Differences and Pastoral Production among the Fulani of Northeastern Senegal, *Africa. Journal of the International African Institute*, 1987. For an example of the pastoralism-equality correlation, see H.K. Schneider, *Livestock and Equality in East-Africa: The Economic Basis for Social Structure*, Bloomington, 1979.

[102] P. Brandström - J. Hultin - J. Lindström, *Aspects of Agro-Pastoralism in East Africa* (Uppsala, 1979) 12; J.W. Sutter, *Cattle and Inequality. Herd Size Differences and Pastoral Production among the Fulani of Northeastern Senegal*, Africa. Journal of the International African Institute, 1987.

[103] P. Spencer, *op. cit.* (1988) 226.

[104] Cfr. M. Talle, *op. cit.*, p. 76.

one who renders it and increases the dependency and subordination of the beneficiary. Rigby mentions none of this.[105]

Nevertheless, there is a sense in which it seems entirely justified to characterize Maasai society as egalitarian. *Te emet enkatai*, say the Maasai. This diction means that even a person who possesses almost nothing may nevertheless one day come to surpass in riches someone who possesses a lot of cattle.[106] It is an affirmation of their anti-fatalist creed, that is, of their faith in the possibility for each person to become rich, even if at the beginning he is unprovided and unlucky by fate or as the result of whatever human intervention, so long as one's own resources of intelligence, foresight, 'management,' and work are used to the maximum. In other words, they firmly believe that one of the fundamental purposes of modern democracy, that of the equality of opportunity for all, is realized in their society. Within the context of the particularities of their specific mode of production, this conviction does not seem to be without basis. The self-reproduction of the essential means of production, cattle, and the unlimited accessibility of the elementary means of production to some extent strengthen its credibility. But we must recognize that this version of egalitarianism strongly calls upon the resources, qualities and efforts of the individual, and that it is hence not without affinities with the understanding of equality prevalent in the ideology of modern capitalist societies. This distantiates us greatly from the essentially anti-capitalist reading of the egalitarianism of the nomadic stock-breeder proposed by Rigby. It is moreover a little surprising that the author feels called upon to articulate a visceral opposition to capitalist ethics among the Maasai and among African herdsmen in general, that is to say precisely among the people who have a mode of subsistence, a system of exchange, and mental attitudes of which the specialists in economic anthropology underline the resemblances and affinities with the capitalist spirit.[107] We are thus disposed to

---

[105] In becoming aware of the disparity revealed by the confrontation of my own field-notes with the description of Rigby, I could not but be reminded of the famous disparity revealed by the works of Redfield and Lewis on Tepoztlán which retained paradigmatic value in anthropological discussion: R. Redfield, *Tepoztlán, a Mexican Village. A Study of Folk Life* (Chicago, 1930); O. Lewis, *Life in a Mexican Village. Tepoztlán Restudied* (Urbana, 1951.) Meanwhile, my reading is not an idiosyncrasy. M. Talle, *op. cit.*, p. 16, writes: "I saw more subjugation than liberation, more conflicts than agreements."

[106] A different proverb *Erisiore enkiteng nabo elukunya olee*, "one single cow is worth the head of a man," expresses the same idea: from one single head of cattle, a dynamic and caring person may build a prosperous house and a filled kraal. Cfr. J.T. Mpaayei, *Inkuti Pukunot ool Maasai* (Oxford, 1954) 39; N. Kipury, *Oral Literature of the Maasai* (Nairobi, 1983) 182.

[107] Z.A. Konczacki, *The Economics of Pastoralism. A Case Study of Sub-Saharan Africa* (London, 1978.)

describe Maasai society as an egalitarian society, though not in the sense that it would lead spontaneously toward an equal distribution of available riches, but rather in that it is a society which guarantees to all adult males equal opportunity for social mobility, and which accepts that all members are constantly exposed to the same risk of bad luck. In the same vein, I am sometimes inclined to suspect that, again in the image of what happens in certain capitalist societies, among the Maasai an egalitarian discourse and etiquette serve partly to mask the factual inequalities and the contradictions resulting from it.[108]

We would like to pause for a moment over the role played by individualism in Maasai culture, focusing especially on the link between this characteristic and the mode of production. We do so because Rigby makes of the link between mode of production and ideology one of the key points of his argument. For example, according to him solidarity, cooperation, and the spirit of community of the Maasai give way to "religious practices and beliefs which engage the whole community."[109] In a certain sense, almost all religious life implies a communal dimension.[110] Hence, to unduly emphasize the almost inevitable social dimension of the Maasai religious practice in order to illustrate the egalitarianism and the communitarianism of their society is a bit too easy and moreover violates the facts. Indeed, if there is anything which differentiates the ritual practice of pastoral people from that of agricultural people, it is that the former insists and concentrates on the individual rather than on the group, which is the focus of the latter. E. Evans-Pritchard expressed himself as follows concerning the religion of the Nuer pastoralists:

> The role of this religion in the regulation of the social life, its structural role, is subsidiary to its role in the regulation of the individual's relations with God, its personal role. The two roles are of different orders and have different functions, and it is the second which has the greater interest for us, for though Nuer religious activity is part of their social life and takes place within it, they conceive it as

---

[108] U. Almagor, "The Ethos of Equality among Dassanetch Age-Peers," in P. Baxter - U. Almagor (eds.), op. cit., p. 70, believes that among the Dassanetch herdsmen the factual inequalities reinforce normative insistence on egalitarianism. About the Waso Borana stock breeders, G. Dahl, op. cit., p. 185, writes: "The egalitarian ideology (...) acts as a screen to conceal real divergences in capital control, recuperative power, and influence between different households."

[109] P. Rigby, op. cit. (1985) 102.

[110] Remember that Durkheim raises the collective aspect to an essential and indispensable dimension of the religious phenomenon: E. Durkheim, Les formes élémentaires de la vie religieuse (Paris, 1960) (1 éd. 1912) 65.

56

expressing essentially a relationship between man and something which lies right outside his society.[111]

W. Goldschmidt does not hesitate to raise the preoccupation with the individual as the specific characteristic of the religion of East African herdsmen[112], and even of that of nomadic stock-raisers in general.[113] This concentration of the ritual practice upon the individual will not be surprising if we remember that the specialists of the pastoral world have come in general to recognize that the tendency toward individualism characterizes the value system and the psychology of nomadic stock-breeders.[114] Someone who knows them well qualifies the Maasai as "stern individualists."[115] This trait is clearly not without a link with the mode of production. The importance of individual initiative and action is crucial in pastoral societies.[116] On the other hand, the local community is relatively unimportant, especially if it is compared to the role which it plays in agrarian societies.

Equally in the area of religious beliefs, Rigby attaches great significance to the relative absence of accusations of witchcraft among the Maasai and among African pastoral societies in general. This observation is well-known and has been related to the absence of agricultural practice and thus of rights to the land as essential means of production. In pastoral societies, the land, grazing grounds, water ponds and salt deposits are not susceptible to appropriation by individuals, kinship groups or local communities. On the other hand, the sedentary

---

[111] E.E. Evans-Pritchard, *Nuer Religion* (Oxford, 1956) 285-286.

[112] W. Goldschmidt, "Introduction," in R.B. Edgerton, *The Individual in Cultural Adaptation. A Study of Four East African Peoples* (Berkeley, 1971) 19.

[113] W. Goldschmidt, "A General Model for Pastoral Social Systems," in C. Lefebure (ed.), *Pastoral Production and Society* (Cambridge - Paris, 1979) 25.

[114] R.B. Edgerton, *op. cit.*, p. 17-18; T. Monod, "Introduction," in T. Monod (ed.), *Pastoralism in Tropical Africa* (London, 1975) 39.

[115] J. Roumeguère-Eberhardt, *op. cit.*, p. 30: "Des individualistes acharnés."

[116] Cfr. R. Edgerton, *op. cit.*, p. 195: "It would appear that independence of action is a pastoral trait, par excellence, and so it should be in an environment where individuals must make many decisions regarding themselves and their herds, usually without recourse to tradition, or group consultation, and, what is more, without delay. In a world where man and his animals are vulnerable to so many threats, life without independent decisions, rapidly made and carried out, would be fragile indeed." Among the Maasai, the truth of these words is imposed upon the male children from an early age in a way which has nothing theoretical. At a very young age, the little boy is sent into the bushes to graze the cattle. In spite of the many and serious dangers to which he is exposed – ferocious buffalos, big game lying in wait for the right moment to take hold of a goat, a sheep or a cow, dangerous elephants, lugubrious hyenas, poisonous snakes, etc. – the boy leaves alone.

agriculturalists are engaged in competition for limited land resources. That which is appropriated by one is subtracted from the usage of the other. This situation encourages recourse to occult means, such as witchcraft practices, destined to undermine the fertility and the well-being of the other.[117] I am inclined to admit that in general and up to a certain point, the more or less frequent practice of witchcraft offers a valuable element of differentiation between nomadic and sedentary societies. On the other hand, I feel more hesitant to rejoin the conclusions which Rigby extracts from this. The relative rarity of accusations of witchcraft among nomadic shepherds constitutes for him an indication and a consequence of the more congenial and cooperative nature of the social relations among the herdsmen, and of the higher social tenor of their system of values. This would thus give evidence to the fact that the pastoral ideology contrasts much more markedly with the colonial ideology of capitalism than does that of the agriculturalists, and would indirectly explain the variation in the degree of permeability manifested by these respective societies with regard to Western culture and religion. If my own record on accusations and practices of witchcraft among the Maasai is sufficiently substantial to confirm that they are less in evidence among this people than among the Kikuyu agriculturalists where I have also worked, still it is too weak to support more detailed conclusions. Luckily, the study of P. Spencer admirably remedies this lack. It shows that if witchcraft is not completely absent from the universe of the *ilmurran*, it is especially upon the world of the elders that it projects its ugly shadow.[118] The author describes it as "a dimension of elderhood."[119] This confirms not only the link between rule of property and witchcraft, but also the existence of an ideological pluralism among the Maasai which coincides with the division between the society of *ilmurran* and *ilpayiani*. In an environment dominated by the elders, that is to say that of kinship and of the village community, witchcraft operates effectively as a major source of disintegration of society.

Nevertheless, the problem remains as to why there are less accusations in the pastoral milieu compared to the agrarian. I think that this is not a difficult question to answer. In describing the processes of removal and of fission at the

---

[117] P.T. Baxter, "Absence Makes the Heart Grow Fonder: Some Suggestions why Witchcraft Accusations are Rare among East African Pastoralists," in M. Gluckman (ed.), *The Allocation of Responsibility* (Manchester, 1972); P.T. Baxter, "Some Consequences of Sedentarization for Social Relationships," in T. Monod (ed.), *Pastoralism in Tropical Africa* (London, 1975); R. Dognin, Sur trois ressorts du comportement peul, *ibidem*; M. Winkelman, "Magico-Religious Practitioner Types and Socioeconomic Conditions," *Behavioral Science Research* (1986.)

[118] P. Spencer, *op. cit.* (1988) 219-220, 224-227, 276.

[119] *Ibidem*, p. 220.

heart of the lineage among Kikuyu cultivators, I emphasized that they are almost always associated with accusations of witchcraft in the sense that they often take place at the end of a long history of accusations and counter-accusations.[120] To change his place of residence constitutes for the Kikuyu farmer an important decision, implying serious economic, social, and psychological consequences. In leaving his original community, he abandons his essential means of production, sacrifices the investments which he has realized, and renounces what has been the ground of security for himself and for his family. It is indeed impossible for him to take the land along with him. Consequently, only in the final resorts will he make recourse to moving, as when the conflictual situation will have become absolutely intolerable. In his understandable concern to avoid or to postpone this ultimate step as long as possible, the farmer will try to repress his negative emotions and, especially, to suspend every hostile action which would be too visible. This is to say that he will come to adopt a secretive disposition and that he will seek alternative, less direct and more veiled ways of expression for his negative and hostile attitudes. The practice of witchcraft is inbuilt in this strategy and its high frequency in the agrarian societies results from the imperative to tolerate to its limits a troubled co-existence. In turn, this imperative is itself derived from the irremovable character of the essential means of production. On the other hand, the pastoral mode of production favors mobility. The herdsman who leaves takes with him without difficulty his essential means of production, his capital, and the basis of his security. The other means of production can be found everywhere and are like the stars: for the use and the joy of all. As soon as the atmosphere becomes poisonous and the first preliminary signs of a conflictual situation become manifest, he is free and able to clear out. After all, moving is part and parcel of his life pattern. The Maasai is linked to neither a particular place nor a community of origin. He easily rejoins another group or establishes elsewhere his own *enkaji* (house). Such a situation facilitates the immediate externalization of frustrations, erodes the inhibition of direct expression of negative emotions, and tends to carry conflicts to the surface without detour.[121] When he feels opposed, the Maasai says what he believes he has to say, gathers his family and his livestock and goes elsewhere. His territory

---

[120] V. Neckebrouck, *op. cit.* (1978) 316-318; *op. cit.* (1983) 374-375, 379.

[121] One hundred years ago, this absence of inhibition struck even an observer who just happened to quickly pass by the Maasai. A. Le Roy, *op. cit.*, p. 431: "Les querelles sont fréquentes et les coups pleuvent souvent."

changes with the cattle.[122] What I am trying to suggest is that the lower number of accusations of witchcraft registered among pastoralists in comparison with the numbers reached among agriculturalists is probably more a function of the more extroverted attitude which the former adopt with regard to frustrations and negative reactions – an attitude in turn linked to their greater mobility – than of whatever higher sociability. More fixed to their piece of land, and thus to the social environment in which this is situated, agriculturalists are almost fatally forced into a strategy of introversion and its occult concomitants, without being able to say that this necessity makes them automatically and in principle less sociable, less inclined to cooperation, more prone to exploitation, and more amenable to capitalism. On the contrary, one could even reverse the argument and hold that the greater dependence of the agriculturalist upon his social milieu which he can desert only at a very high price, forces him more toward collaboration and compromise, than the nomadic herdsman who can detach himself from his environment at far less cost.

The lack of attention given to the divergences existing within the ideological universe, and to the distance between professed culture and lived culture, considerably weakens the explanatory weight attributed by Rigby to the ideological factor which is, according to him, inextricably linked to the mode of production. But there is more. The author is right to deny all differentiation in the fundamental attitude of the Maasai with respect to their pastoral way of life to which, notwithstanding the oppositions and the different strategies, they all remain profoundly attached. It is precisely this conservative choice which needs to be explained. Rigby states that the Maasai rejected Christianity because this seemed to them to be linked to an ideology which was radically incompatible with an ethics dictated in an imperative way by their specific mode of production. It is difficult to see how this theory accounts for the conservative option itself when one knows that, as we have shown above, concretely the Maasai could indeed have made recourse to alternative modes of production. I add that they have in

---

[122] The relation between ease of mobility and reduction of the frequency of accusations of witchcraft has been observed among other nomadic herdsmen: I.M. Lewis, *A Pastoral Democracy* (London, 1961) 26; P. Spencer, *The Samburu. A Study of Gerontocracy in a Nomadic Tribe* (Berkeley, 1965); P.H. Gulliver, *The Family Herds. A Study of Two Pastoral Tribes in East Africa: The Jie and Turkana* (London, 1955); P.H. Gulliver, "Nomadic Movements: Causes and Implications," in T. Monod (ed.), *op. cit.*; R.B. Edgerton, *op. cit.*; W. Goldschmidt, "Independence as an Element in Pastoral Social Systems," *Anthropological Quarterly* (1971); W. Goldschmidt, *art. cit.* (1979); W. Goldschmidt, "Career Reorientation and Institutional Adaptation in the Process of Natural Sedentarization," in P.C. Salzman (ed.), *When Nomads Settle. Processes of Sedentarization as Adaptation and Response* (New York, 1980.)

fact practised them. The Maasai ideology is radically opposed to the practice of agriculture because the land constitutes a resource which must remain universally accessible, as Rigby with good reason reminds us.[123] That which he seems to ignore, or that which he at least fails to state, is that in the past this has not prevented the Maasai from giving themselves over in certain circumstances to this mode of production, free to return to the pastoral way of life as soon as circumstances allowed it.[124] Just as this has not kept certain subgroups from installing themselves in a more or less permanent way in one or the other form of alternative production.[125] These facts are food for thought. One may wonder if they do not force us to consider and to interpret certain contemporary facts in a different perspective, such as that of the passage to sedentarization and to agriculture effected by certain Maasai groups of our day. We are accustomed to speaking in this context of a spectacular change or fundamental mutation while, in reality, it may instead be a phase of a *totally traditional* oscillation between two alternative institutionalized possibilities.[126] Some years ago, I called attention to this notion of institutionalized alternatives to account for certain phenomena which were commonly identified as drastic cultural changes.[127] I did not know then that a few years earlier, P.C. Salzman had already applied this model to the analysis of social change in the world of nomadic herdsmen.[128] That which we would thus like to place in evidence is that both the diachronic and the synchronic study of pastoral societies, including that of the Maasai, reveals that nomadism and sedentism, the pastoral and the agricultural way of life, may not constitute these two entirely incompatible types, these two completely and radically opposite universes which conceptualizations in the manner of *ideal-type* and models of classification pleasing to the soul, but

---

[123] P. Rigby, *op. cit.* (1985) 101.

[124] See on this topic, J.L. Berntsen, "Economic Variations among Maa-Speaking Peoples," in B.A. Ogot (ed.), *Ecology and History in East Africa* (Nairobi, 1979.)

[125] Cfr. J.G. Galaty, "Pollution and Pastoral Antipraxis: the Issue of Maasai Inequality," *American Ethnologist* (1979) 803: "Maasai society (...) surprisingly includes several subgroups that are primarily characterized by forms of nonideal praxis."

[126] Other alternative forms which have been adopted include hunting and ironworking.

[127] Notably, to interpret the conversion of the Kikuyu to Christianity: V. Neckebrouck, *op. cit.* (1983) 280-291.

[128] P.C. Salzman, Ideology and Change in Middle Eastern Tribal Societies, *Man*, (1978); P.C. Salzman, "Processes of Sedentarization as Adaptation and Response," in P.C. Salzman (ed.), *When Nomads Settle* (New York, 1980.) See also, E. Marx, "The Ecology and Politics of Nomadic Pastoralists in the Middle East," in W. Weissleder (ed.), *The Nomadic Alternative. Modes and Models of Interaction in the African-Asian Deserts and Steppes* (Den Haag - Paris, 1978.)

ultimately of little conformity to reality, may tend to propose.[129] One important consequence of the foregoing is that it is not always without danger to character-ize and to understand a society in terms of what Herskovits called his 'cultural foyer',[130] or of what Rigby describes as his "dominant ideological instance," referring in the case of the Maasai to the age class organization.[131] Such approaches encourage an analysis of society elaborated on the basis of a suppos-edly omnipresent underlying structure from which all aspects of life and culture are directly or indirectly derived. This type of description leads to an image of a solidly integrated, highly predetermined, quasi-invariable and little changing society. It tends, moreover, to ignore or to eliminate from description the elements which do not harmonize with the perspective of the 'focal point' or of the 'dominant structure.' To account for these would force the researcher to present an image of society which is much more diversified, integrating aspects which are dysfunctional, less uniform and less homogenous, more flexible, more nuanced, and more subjected to change. One may wonder if Rigby is not the prisoner of a type of interpretation of Maasai society which is thereby challenged. His insistence on the indestructible union between mode of production and ideology points in this direction. This is further corroborated by his silence on the periodic revitalization of alternative modes of subsistence observable in Maasai society; his forgetfulness, at least in as far as the practical consequences are concerned, of the impact of the kinship structure and his negligence regarding the disparity between ideological conceptions and the realities of concrete exist-ence. In fact, one may wonder whether the type of society envisaged by Rigby would be *überhaupt* susceptible to change.[132] In this case, rather than posing a problem, Maasai conservatism would rather pertain to the normal order of things. It is in the perspective of a reading of the Maasai society as ours, which integrates the elements neglected by Rigby, that the question of the impermeability of the people to the Western religion becomes really *fragwürdig*. It is only when one knows that a particular ideology does not prevent a people from deviating from it according to circumstances, from negotiating it according to constraints, from manipulating it according to the interests of the moment,

---

[129] P.C. Salzman, *art. cit.* (1980) 13: "The shift between nomadism and sedentism, and between pastoralism and agriculture, as a current circumstance and set of activities, is in many respects not such an absolute break as it might seem *prima facie*."

[130] M.J. Herskovits, *Les bases de l'anthropologie culturelle* (Paris, 1967) 236-255.

[131] P. Rigby, *op. cit.* (1988) 98.

[132] As so many critics of the functionalist-structuralist and Marxist conceptions of society have brought to light. These theories do allow for certain forms of change, but not for the most import-ant in the case of the first, and not for the most common in the case of the latter.

that an interrogation such as that of the present study acquires meaning. The Maasai are conscious of the contradiction between their ideology of egalitarianism and solidarity, tributary to the structure of the age class organization, and the concessions made to the particularism linked with the kinship structure. And they attempt to use this contradiction to their own advantage, in which they are doubtless no different from the majority of people all over the world. According to our experience, the habitual scenario of the behavior of an adult and married Maasai takes the following pattern. That which dominates are the interests of the *pater familias*. It will thus normally be these interests which will be pursued, if necessary at the cost of the exigencies of the official ideology. Nevertheless, in certain circumstances, the very interest of the patriarch and of his family may require submission to the imperatives of the ideology which, as such, are then transformed from constraints to opportunities. In these cases, the chief of the family, after having weighed pros and cons, will not usually have much difficulty in practising complaisance. Finally, in still other circumstances the application of the imperatives of ideology *by the others* with regard to him may be to his benefit and even become a condition of his survival as herdsman. It is clear that he then will be the first to call upon the egalitarian tradition, upon the sacred duty of solidarity and demand its application.[133]

It is time to conclude this discussion. The argument that the reception of Christianity in the particular form in which it presented itself in East-Africa would have introduced a stratification in the Maasai society is not salient. Differences sometimes explicit on the level of economic well-being have in fact never been absent and the rich (*ilkarsisi*) and poor (*ilaisinak*) have always coexisted in society.[134] The consideration that the insertion of the Maasai into capitalist economy would have delivered them to poverty is not more peremptory, since it has not prevented many other peoples from showing themselves receptive to change in general and to Christianity in particular. Rigby's affirmation, according to which the Maasai would have been in this more shrewd than their neighbors,[135] is not corroborated by any real proof. The history of protest of the majority of Bantu people against despoiling and exploitation very often goes back to the beginnings of colonization. These people made recourse to

---

[133] The same pattern may be discerned with regard to other aspects of Maasai ideology, such as for example the division of work between the sexes, the attitude with regard to the practice of agriculture and the consumption of its products.

[134] Cfr. supra and R.D. Waller, *Economic and Social Relations in the Central Rift Valley: The Maa-Speakers and Their Neighbors in the Nineteenth Century*, Unpublished Paper, cited by J. Iliffe, *op. cit.* (1987) 68.

[135] P. Rigby, *op. cit.* (1985) 120.

Christianity, and to Western education and culture with the hope of using them to articulate their protests and to reach their goals. The Maasai did not adopt this perspective. The difference resides not in the fact of having perceived or not the colonial threat, but in the way of defending oneself against it. Moreover, collaboration with the colonial system would have been able to seduce certain sections of the population. The Maasai did not ignore that among their Bantu neighbors, certain lineages and clans drew from it certain economic and social benefits, assuring them even until today a dominant position in society. Why did they react by rejecting the same opportunities which the Bantu have only been too happy to exploit? Finally, if Rigby is convinced that it is the link with Western capitalism which rendered Christianity unacceptable to the Maasai, how does he explain the fact that the people have never showed themselves more receptive to Islam? This religion is not corrupted by the ideology of Western capitalism and is usually considered to favor solidarity, cooperation, egalitarianism, and the communal spirit. While the author seems to be aware of this question,[136] he scrupulously avoids answering it. This much must be acknowledged: with regard to all of this, the conscious and deliberate, massive and obstinate engagement of the Maasai in the conservative option remains fundamentally unexplained.

---

[136] *Ibidem*, p. 96.

SOCIALIZATION

At the end of this survey, we can only reiterate what we affirmed from the start: if the different theories explaining the conservative commitment of the Maasai and, indirectly, the failure of the Christian missions among them are of unequal value, none of them can at bottom really convince us. Perhaps their common weakness is that they are all committed to a kind of theoretical monoculture. By this, I understand that they all tend to singularize and privilege a particular factor from which they expect all necessary explanatory power. Human situations being more often complex than simple, would it not be more desirable to abandon such a unidimensional perspective in favor of etiological models which give an important role to the conjunction and mutual interaction of elements? Could not social science draw inspiration from the wisdom of a great novelist: "Who can say how things come about? Nothing comes from a single cause, but from many."[137] In discussing the ecological argument, we advanced that the latter seemed to be corroborated by recent studies on social change among the Kamba.[138] In reality, and in spite of appearances, it is highly improbable that the physical environment constitutes the only variable responsible for the differentiated socio-cultural evolution of the Kamba districts. To adequately explain the phenomenon, it seems that social factors have to be taken into equal consideration.[139]

Another deficiency which affects at least a certain number of the proposed theories is their tautological reasoning. Even some of the more elaborate theories do not escape this defect; the development of a more sophisticated theoretical discourse merely defers its exposure. Reduced to its simplest expression, the explication of Rigby, for example, comes down to the view that the Maasai refused Christianity because they discerned in it a threat to the specific pastoral system which integrates in an exemplary way their mode of production, social

---

[137] K. Hamsun, *Growth of the Soil* (New York, 1973 (1 ed. 1917)) 408.
[138] See notes ns. 65 and 66.
[139] G.C. Mutiso, "Kitui Ecosystem, Integration and Change," in B.A. Ogot (ed.), *op. cit.*

praxis, and ideological structure; in other words because of their fidelity to the pastoral way of life. To this we have no objection except to say that it leaves us completely in obscurity concerning the factors explaining this unshakable and universal loyalty. It is indeed there that seems to reside the fundamental residual and intrinsic difficulty of several of the proposed models, which the protagonists have not been able, or have not tried to resolve. As soon as this is perceived, one is strongly tempted to take refuge in one thesis or the other which is not affected by the tautological vice, for example that of prosperity, that of isolation, that of unadapted acculturation, or that of the ecological argument. Unfortunately, the deficiency of each of these theories has been exposed. Two or three lame together do not guarantee the unlimping walk of an upright body. It is not in this sense that one should understand our plea for renunciation of a theoretical monoculture. The attention given to the conjunction and interaction of factors which we advocate will have to deploy more subtle ways to gain respectability. But to reach this end, we must introduce a new element of which the importance has thus far been rarely recognized. The help which it may provide the search for an answer to that which we have called the residual question seems funda-mental to us.

It has been known for a long time that stock raising nomads are among the people most difficult to bring to open themselves up to Christianity and to Western civilization in general. In this sense, the Maasai are only a particular illustration of a more global given. Our own first encounter with the Maasai goes back to 1969. In spite of the ephemeral and superficial character of this contact, I was able to note that the members of this people are profoundly attached to their way of life, that they derive satisfaction and pride from it to a degree that I had not observed among the different African agricultural peoples with whom I was familiar for much longer, that they had absolutely no doubt of the superior-ity of their culture, and that they exhibited a sharp and elevated sense of their personal value as well as of the distinguished nobility of the pastoral vocation. These traits caught the eye to that degree that one would have to be blind not to see them. This initial impression was confirmed and reinforced at each new encounter. In the meanwhile, the reading of the texts of the first explorers and missionaries of the region taught me that this discovery had been made long before me.[140] Frequentation of the larger ethnographical literature made me conscious of the fact that the specific traits which I discerned among the Maasai in fact constituted traits recurring to a more or less accentuated degree among pastoral peoples all over the world. Hence, I felt authorized to conclude that these constituted qualities which were concomitant to or resulting from the pastoral mode of existence itself. In a statistically significant way, stock raising nomads thus combine a marked resistance to Christianity with an equally pronounced consciousness of the superior dignity of their culture.

It is of course tempting to establish a causal link between these two common characteristics, and this has not been avoided by some students of Maasai society. I rejected this way of proceeding because of the implied recourse to tautological reasoning. However, with time, the intensity of the feeling of pastoral identity appeared to me to be ever more a kind of *fait primitif* of Maasai thinking. The suggestion of Galaty imposed itself more and more upon me as the adequate expression of the truth: "Maasai society is most adequately grasped through the image of its intense pride in the pastoral ideal."[141] I thus ended convinced that the statistically significant concomitance of the three elements – pastoral nomadism, exacerbated ethnocentrism and strong resistance to Christianity – provides an indication of which one must take account. It is only important to avoid the circular reasoning by pushing ahead the real question. That is to say, instead of remaining content with explaining the conservative reflex by the sense of exceptionally pronounced cultural superiority of the Maasai, one must also try to answer the question of the origins of the latter.

In 1987, on the glacial heights of a small Andean village of Peru, I encountered a particularly obstinate anthropological problem raised by the local situation. One day, I was brought to ask myself whether the solution to the enigma which was defying me should not be sought in the direction of the mode of socialization of the young children operating in the local community. I still do not have a definite answer to this question. But that has no importance for our present purpose. However, my reflections on this subject mentally brought me back to the Maasai. The idea suddenly dawned on me that, even though I was aware of the constitutive links between the genesis of ethnocentrism and the

---

[140] I cannot resist the temptation to quote at least one of these ancient testimonies because it discerns even in the young Maasai children the above mentioned trait. A. Le Roy, *op. cit.*, p. 154: "Ils me regardent d'un air ressemblant beaucoup au dédain, un peu à l'intérêt, pas du tout à la peur, l'air de jeunes Européens de 'bonnes familles' qui, dans le parc du château paternel, verraient un beau jour surgir un petit bonhomme de mauvaise mine."

[141] J.G. Galaty, *art. cit.*, p. 803.

process of enculturation[142], in my reflection *on this people* I had never established an immediate rapport nor a correlation between the modalities of socialization and the intensity of the ethnocentric sentiment. Moreover, as far as I could tell, nobody else seemed to have considered doing so. This is the path which my reasoning then followed: The degree of attachment to one's own culture is, at least in part, a function of the intensity of the sense of superiority cultivated with regard to this culture. Normally this sense is itself a product of the process of enculturation. Hence, it is useful and pertinent to examine whether, among the Maasai, this process presents certain modalities capable of explaining the unusual intensity of the ethnocentric consciousness and, thereby, the conservative commitment of the people.

Later, in reexamining my fieldnotes from this perspective, two elements emerged, one relating to the content of the socializing discourse, and the other concerning the treatment inflicted on the young male child during the period of his education preceding initiation. The superiority of the pastoral way of life is constantly inculcated in the young child. Unable to enter here into details, we limit ourselves to mentioning the facts in a general and synthetic way. An impressive number of myths, stories, and legends explicitly or implicitly carries the teaching of the preeminence of the pastoral life. The numerous rites through which the child passes at a young age express the same idea and contribute, with all the power carried by ritual language, maintaining and reinforcing it. This is not to mention the daily discourse which is literally peppered with references to the excellence of the pastoral way of life in general and of that of the Maasai in particular. At the time of initiation all this is brought to a paroxysm in a highly dramatized way. It is important to add that both daily and mythological discourse insist upon the necessity of paying the price for meriting the dignity of belonging to a pastoral people, and exalt the courage, endurance, aggressiveness and independence without which this belonging is considered impossible. The rituals serve partly to allow to facilitate acquisition of these qualities or to test the degree of realization of them. The infliction of pain which must be mastered plays an important part in these rituals. Here are a few examples. At the age of about four, the inferior incisors are torn out with the help of a knife. If they grow back, they are again removed. The small boys are encouraged to burn themselves all along their limbs with burning hot coals, competing to see who best withstands this

---

[142] The term enculturation was coined by M.J. Herskovits, *op. cit.*, p. 54, to refer to the process of socialization in human societies. It must not be confused with the term inculturation which is of theological origin. It is thus incorrect to state that "l'inculturation est un néologisme forgé par le professeur américain Herskovits," as does M. Hebga, *Dépassements* (Paris, 1978) 57.

test. A little later they are tattooed on the belly and on the arms by means of a needle and a knife. Holes in the superior cartilage of the ear are pierced with a red hot iron and a piece of flesh is cut from the lobes. The holes are subsequently maintained and enlarged with a piece of wood, ivory, or metal which is put there and which is made increasingly bigger. These interventions are known to be very painful. The Maasai male initiation involves a type of circumcision which is very complicated and extremely painful. All this initiatory violence is not without purpose. It contributes to preparing the Maasai for the pastoral life which is difficult and harsh.[143] From morning to evening he is exposed to the inclemencies of the weather, to the blazing sun and to whipping storms, to clouds of dust and to biting winds. His days are long, tiring, and often lonely. He must every moment be prepared to confront wild animals and armed thieves who attack the flock. These threats sometimes present themselves suddenly and presuppose, in a man often relying only on himself, an immediate and almost instinctual perception of danger, the capacity to develop a strategy of defense in a few fractions of a second, and the courage and ability to effectively ward off attack. Moreover, the ethos inculcated by this socialization makes certain that he can distantiate himself from these attacks only at the risk of carrying for the rest of his days the inalienable stigma of cowardice.

The second element of socialization needing mention here must also be understood in function of the needs of pastoral life. It concerns the treatment of the male child by paternal authority. I observed above that the Maasai child is from very early on familiarized with pastoral tasks. It is normal to see a little boy of six or seven years old leave the paternal kraal alone in order to take charge of a flock of calves. A few years later, he will without hesitation be entrusted with the cattle. The responsibility weighing on his young shoulders is immense, for things may go wrong in a thousand and one ways. I have often observed some of these children left completely to themselves and entangled in situations in which, full adult as I was, I could never have resolved so well. An entire volume could be filled on the vicissitudes of the concrete pastoral life, of which the hard demands are constantly and naively underestimated by the occasional observer. That which is relevant here is to note that the paternal reaction to every omission or negligence by the child of which the father of the family becomes aware is, whether or not the child is guilty and whether or not there are disastrous consequences for the whole livestock or one single animal, disproportionate and frightening, by European standards. The culprit is very severely

---

[143] The relationship between the ritual infliction of physical pain and the hardness of life among nomadic herdsmen is known: W. Goldschmidt, *art. cit.* (1979) 25.

punished, hit without mercy, and deprived of food for some length of time. Moreover, he is deeply humiliated by reproaches which question his sense of the value of cattle, his pastoral vocation and dispositions, and his ability to become a real Maasai. I have personally known several adults who admitted that, in their youth, they would have preferred to flee rather than confront paternal wrath after entering the house with an animal with a broken leg or without having recuperated a lost animal. It must be underlined that the severity of paternal sanction is meant to impose upon the malleable spirit of the child the conviction that a lapse in the pastoral domain equals a complete failure, that it is a matter of life or death, that the only choice which presents itself to him is that between a dignified existence as Maasai and the fall into the nothingness of laziness and the vagabond life, into which all other life projects are explicitly or implicitly assimilated.

It is time to come to that to which all of this has led me. Presented synthetically, my argument boils down to the following: The pastoral life demands from those who practice it a virility, an aggressiveness, an endurance and a disposition to confront suffering, dangers, and solitude superior to those demanded by the other modes of production in non-Western societies. To guarantee the reproduction of a society of which the way of life is unable to avoid such exigencies, it is indispensable that its members develop exceptionally strong motivations. The acquisition of these motivations cannot be effected outside a process of enculturation which simultaneously prepares adequately for the specific trials inherent in the mode of production and exacerbates the ethnocentric consciousness. We have tried to show in a schematic way that the Maasai socialization effectively fulfils these two conditions. As for the originality of my discovery, of which my extreme naivety for a time convinced me, I have had to lower my tone. I have since come to know that, in the footsteps of his professor, G. Engerrand, W. Goldschmidt had already searched in the same direction. He had even formulated the daring conclusion that in the absence of their specific type of socialization, pastoral people would purely and simply cease to be pastoralists.[144]

I am thus inclined to interpret the unconditional attachment of the Maasai to their pastoral way of life as a direct consequence of the particular modalities of their system of socialization. I have good reasons for believing that this reading which, I admit, fatally constitutes the product of an exterior viewpoint, nevertheless closely rejoins an intuition which seems to have occupied also those

---

[144] W. Goldschmidt, *art. cit.* (1979) 26-27.

concerned. Indeed, that to which the Maasai have always [in certain regions even until this very day] offered the strongest resistance is the enrolment of their children in Western missionary, or government schools. Wouldn't this be because they suspect that, away from the constraints of socialization, these children would indeed verify the diagnosis of Goldschmidt? Of course, the recruitment of children for the schools has provoked resentment in the majority of African societies. But in agricultural societies this phenomenon has remained limited to the beginning of the era of colonization. Among the Maasai, it was not only prolonged well beyond this initial period, it has also been felt much more deeply as an intolerable interference. Basing himself on the sources of government archives and on fieldwork, R.L. Tignor writes:

> Few societies reacted with such intensity to this innovation as the Maasai(...). It is difficult for an outsider to grasp the full measure of their opposition. Informants were not clear about these matters. They likened schoolgoing to an unbearable loss such as the death or enslavement of children. They felt that if children went to school they would be lost forever to Maasai society.[145]

---

[145] R.L. Tignor, art. cit., p. 281. Cfr. H.R. Ole Kulet, Is It Possible? (Nairobi, 1971) 5-17; Tepilit Ole Saitoti, The Worlds of a Maasai Warrior. An Autobiography (Berkeley - Los Angeles, 1988) 25-26.

FINAL DETERMINATIONS

One will have measured the distance which separates our approach from the tautological explanation of conservatism by nature, by mentality. Not only did we replace the appeal to nature with recourse to cultural factors but, in bringing the specific characteristics of Maasai enculturation to light, we have also answered the question of why, as opposed to that which happened among so many other ethnic groups, ethnocentrism led this people to the rejection of acculturation. Can the analysis which we have proposed be qualified as causal? Must it be understood as an explanation or as an interpretation? Since the borderline between these two types of analysis are not as neat as it was thought but tend to blur, it is difficult to answer this question with a simple 'yes' or 'no.' We do not need to enter here into a discussion which is obviously complex and complicated.[146] I wish only to specify that if the causal qualification evokes an image of the Maasai reacting to enculturation in a way in which non-human agents respond to factors which make them act, that is to say if it implies a purely mechanistic understanding of the influence of socialization, I reject its application to the proposed explanation. This is to avoid committing a double error. First, that of sacrificing the liberty of human agents in favor of an unreflective determinism. The Maasai are not prisoners of their socialization to the point of being deprived of all possibility of avoiding its impact. The fact that the large majority of a people which highly values personal liberty has not used this possibility of escape nevertheless needs explanation. I believe that the specific modalities of pastoral socialization have not been foreign to this massive and constant disaffection with regard to acculturation. But the refusal to interpret this causal influence in terms of a deterministic model simultaneously allows for awareness of exceptions and avoids anticipation. The second mistake lurking

---

[146] R.W. Wyllie, "On the Rationality of the Devout Opposition," *Journal of Religion in Africa* (1980); R.A. Segal, "In Defense of Reductionism," *Journal of the American Academy of Religion* (1983); R.A. Segal, "Response to Blasi and Nelson," *Journal for the Scientific Study of Religion* (1986); R.A. Segal, *Religion and the Social Sciences. Essays on the Confrontation* (Atlanta, 1989) 14-20, 67-74; R.A. Segal, "Religionist and Social Scientific Strategies," *Religion* (1989.)

behind the use of a mechanistic conception is that of emptying the concept of causality of the density of significance with which it is charged in being transposed into a human milieu. To the extent to which enculturation is a question of interiorization of norms and values, it is clear that its impact cannot be analyzed exclusively in terms of causes in the strict sense of the term, but it should also be done in terms of intentions, objectives, motives, and reasons. In other words, it cannot be isolated or really discerned from the activity by which the subject grants meaning and signification to his behavior. In order to decide whether an analysis in those terms must or can still be qualified as causal, the main concern is to know whether intentions, objectives, motives, and reasons, as also underlying valorizations, may or may not be legitimately called (mental) causes. As we have said before, we do not wish here to enter into this debate.

Meanwhile, the socialization seems to provide much of the theses which have here passed in review, with the indispensable complementary explicative element, the absence of which renders them limited. Finally, in speaking of complement, I suggest that the theory of socialization permits us to avoid the other deficiency of the presented theories: that which I have called theoretical monoculture. Indeed, if we are persuaded that the modalities of socialization play a preponderant and decisive role in the genesis of Maasai conservatism, we do not therefore feel obliged to conclude to the total lack of pertinence, to the total futility of the considerations advanced by several of the theories which we have here reviewed. That would imply surrendering myself to the temptation of a theoretical monoculture which I have just denounced. I merely feel justified in maintaining that the part of truth which they may hold can only be acknowledged at the price of also recognizing their partial, unilateral, and incomplete character, and of an insertion in a larger explanatory frame which necessarily also integrates the intensity of the motivation to persist at all price as nomadic stock raisers. With regard to the many sacrifices which this way of life implies, such a motivational intensity could not reach the required temperature unless it is maintained by the fire of an appropriate practice of enculturation. Revised in such a way, the different theses will be able to gain credibility making them worthy of a new examination. If one can predict that some will certainly not survive the test, still I like to believe that the majority will reveal themselves as complementary perspectives, seen from different viewpoints, rather than as incompatible and irreconcilable approaches. We cannot here provide the demonstration for all these theories. Moreover, that is unnecessary. One example will suffice to illustrate that some would gain in explanatory potential if they would remit isolation of themselves from certain others. We have already shown that, if in itself the avoidance of a decisive military confrontation does not explain anything, still it is not without interest that it has allowed the Maasai to maintain intact their warrior organization and hence a social structure based on the complementary opposition of age classes. Nevertheless this element itself becomes really pertinent only to the extent to which the institution of the *ilmurran* reinforces the impact of a socialization of which it constitutes simultaneously the summit, the main instrument and the privileged location. If the Western school was so mistrusted, abhorred, and feared by the Maasai, this was precisely because it functioned as the great alternative to the *manyata*. Of course the explicational pertinence does not lie in the socialization as such, as universal institution. It is the particular characteristics of the pastoral enculturation which are relevant. Evidently, these are linked to the mode of production and, at least in certain regions, to the physical environment. In themselves, however, neither the mode of production nor the ecological conditions arrive at adequately accounting for the Maasai conservatism. This closes the circle and sends us back again to the mode of socialization.

That to which our survey has led us is thus less the presentation of a new theory which would stand beside the others annihilating them all, than the discovery of a cornerstone which none would be able to reject without punishment, of a kind of pivot around which all seem to me to have to henceforth articulate themselves. In short, in debates such as that which has been developed here, anthropology seems to be less equipped to express indisputable solutions in a positive or peremptory way than to discard, criticize, or nuance responses which present themselves as such. In the words of C. Geertz: "Anthropology is a science whose progress is marked less by a perfection of consensus than by a refinement of debate. What gets better is the precision with which we vex each other."[147]

---

[147] G. Geertz, *The Interpretation of Cultures* (New York, 1973) 19.

BIBLIOGRAPHY

Only the books and articles actually cited in the text have been listed in this bibliography.

ALMAGOR, U. *The Ethos of Equality among Dassanetch Age-Peers*, in:
P. BAXTER - U. ALMAGOR (eds.), London, 1978.

ARAP NGEY, S. *Nandi Resistance to the Establishment of British Administration*, Hadith II, Nairobi, 1970.

AYOADE, J. *Time in Yoruba Thought*, in: R. WRIGHT (ed.), Washington, 1977.

BARREAU, J. *Ecologie*, in: R. CRESWELL (ed.), Paris, 1975.

BARRETT, D.B. *World Christian Encyclopaedia*, London, 1982.

BASCOM, W.R. - HERSKOVITS, M.J. (eds.), *Continuity and Change in African Cultures*, Chicago, 1959.

BAXTER, P. *Absence Makes the Heart Grow Fonder: Some Suggestions Why Witchcraft Accusations Are Rare among East African Pastoralists*, in:
M. GLUCKMAN (ed.), Manchester, 1972.

————, *Some Consequences of Sedentarization for Social Relationships*, in:
T. MONOD (ed.), London, 1975.

————, *Boran Age-Sets - a Puzzle or a Maze?*, in: P. BAXTER -
U. ALMAGOR (eds.), London, 1978.

———— - ALMAGOR, U. (eds.), *Age, Generation and Time. Some Features of East African Age Organization*, London, 1978.

BENTSEN, C. *Maasai Days. A First-Hand Account of Life in an African Village*, London, 1990.

BERDICHEWSKY, B. (ed.), *Anthropology and Social Change in Rural Areas*, Den Haag - Paris - New York, 1979.

BERNTSEN, J.L. *Pastoralism, Raiding and Prophets: Maasailand in the Nineteenth Century*, Doctoral Thesis, University of Wisconsin, 1979.

————, *Economic Variations among Maa-Speaking Peoples*, in: B.A. OGOT (ed.), Nairobi, 1979.

BOHANNAN, P. - DALTON, G. (eds.), *Markets in Africa*, Evanston, 1962.

BONTE, P. *Cattle for God: An Attempt at a Marxist Analysis of the Religion of East African Herdsmen*, Social Compass, 1975.

BOUFFARD, L. *La perspective future chez les Africains*, Revue d'Ethnopsychologie, 1982.

BRANDSTRÖM, P. - HULTIN, J. - LINDSTRÖM, J. *Aspects of Agro-Pastoralism in East Africa*, Uppsala, 1979.

BRAUDEL, F. *Grammaire des civilisations*, Paris, 1988.

BUCHER, H. *Spirits and Power: An Analysis of Shona Cosmology*, Cape Town, 1980.

BÜHLMANN, W. *The Church of the Future. A Model for the Year 2001*, Maryknoll - Melbourne - Slough, 1986.

CRESWELL, R. (ed.), *Eléments d'ethnologie*. Vol. II, Paris, 1975.

DAHL, G. - HJORT, A. *Having Herds. Pastoral Herd Growth and Household Economy*, Stockholm, 1976.

————, *Ecology and Equality: The Boran case*, in: C. LEFEBURE (ed.), Cambridge - Paris, 1979.

————, *Suffering Grass. Subsistence and Society of Waso Borana*, Stockholm, 1979.

DE MAHIEU, W. *Le temps dans la culture komo*, Africa. Journal of the International African Institute, 1973.

DEMPSEY, J. *Mission on the Nile*, London, 1955.

d'HERTEFELT, M. *Political Anthropology*, Leuven, 1990.

DOGNIN, R. *Sur trois ressorts du comportement peul*, in: T. MONOD (ed.), London, 1975.

DONOVAN, V.J. *Christianity Rediscovered. An Epistle from the Masai*, Notre Dame, 1978.

DURKHEIM, E. *Les formes élémentaires de la vie religieuse. Le système totémique en Australie*, Paris, 1960 (1 ed. 1912).

EDGERTON, R.B. *The Individual in Cultural Adaptation. A Study of Four East African Peoples*, Berkeley, 1971.

EVANS-PRITCHARD, E.E. *Nuer Religion*, Oxford, 1956.

FASHOLE-LUKE, E. (ed.), *Christianity in Independent Africa*, London, 1978.

FISCHER, G.A. *Das Maasailand*, Hamburg, 1885.

FOSBROOKE, H.A. *The Maasai Age-Group System as a guide to Tribal Chronology*, African Studies, 1956.

GALATY, J. *Pollution and Pastoral Antipraxis: The Issue of Maasai Inequality*, American Ethnologist, 1979.

——————— - ARONSON, D. - SALZMAN, P.C. (eds.), *L'avenir des peuples pasteurs*, Ottawa, 1983.

GEERTZ, C. *The Interpretation of Cultures*, New York, 1973.

GLUCKMAN, M. *Custom and Conflict in Africa*, Oxford, 1956.

———————, *Politics, Law and Ritual in Tribal Society*, Oxford, 1965.

———————, (ed.), *The Allocation of Responsability*, Manchester, 1972.

GODELIER, M. *Horizons, trajets marxistes en anthropologie*, Paris, 1973.

GOLDSCHMIDT, W. *Introduction*, in: R.B. EDGERTON, Berkeley, 1971.

———————, *Independence as an Element in Pastoral Social Systems*, Anthropological Quarterly, 1971.

———————, *A general Model for Pastoral Social Systems*, in: C. LEFEBURE (ed.), Cambridge - Paris, 1979.

———————, *Career Reorientation and Institutional Adaptation in the Process of Natural Sedentarization*, in: P.C. SALZMAN (ed.), New York, 1980.

GULLIVER, P.H. *The Family Herds. A Study of Two Pastoral Tribes in East Africa: The Jie and Turkana*, London, 1955.

———————, *The Evolution of Arusha Trade*, in: P. BOHANNAN - G. DALTON (eds.), Evanston, 1962.

———————, *Social Control in an African Society. A Study of the Arusha, Agricultural Masai of Northern Tanganyika*, London, 1963.

———————, *The Conservative Commitment in Northern Tanzania. The Arusha and Masai*, in: P.H. GULLIVER (ed.), London, 1969.

———————, (ed.), *Tradition and Transition in East Africa*, London, 1969.

HAMSUN, K. *Growth of the Soil*, New York, 1973 (1 ed. 1917).

HEBGA, M. *Dépassements*, Paris, 1978.

HELLBOM, A.B. *Sociocultural Changes Resulting from Road Construction in Areas of Difficult Access*, in: B. BERDICHEWSKY (ed.), Den Haag - Paris - New York, 1979.

HERSKOVITS, M.J. *Les bases de l'anthropologie culturelle*, Paris, 1967.

HOTCHKISS, W.R. *Then and Now in Kenya Colony*, New York, 1937.

HUNTINGFORD, G.W. *The Southern Nilo-Hamites*, London, 1953.

HUTCHINS, P. *Continuity and Change among the Maasai People*, M.A. Thesis, Fuller Theological Seminary, 1987.

HUXLEY, E. *The Sorcerer's Apprentice*, London, 1949.

ILIFFE, J. *The African Poor. A History*, Cambridge, 1987.

JACOBS, A. *Maasai Pastoralism in Historical Perspective*, in: T. MONOD (ed.), London, 1975.

JAMES, L. *The Kenya Masai. A Nomadic People under Modern Administration*, Africa. Journal of the International African Institute, 1939.

JULIEN, P. *Zonen van Cham. Onder Oost-Afrikaanse Steppevolken*, Amsterdam, 1958.

KAGAMA, A. *Aperception empirique du temps et conception de l'histoire dans la pensée bantu*, in: P. RICOEUR (ed.), Paris, 1975.

KARP, I. - BIRD, C.S. (eds.), *Explorations in African Systems of Thought*, Bloomington, 1980.

KENYA RANGELANDS ENVIRONMENT MONITORING UNIT, *Population Stocking Rates and Distribution of Wildlife and Livestock on the Mara and Loita Plains*, Nairobi, 1980.

KHAZANOV, A.M. *Characteristic Features of Nomadic Communities in the Eurasian Steppes*, in: W. WEISSLEIDER (ed.), Den Haag - Paris, 1978.

KING, K. *African Students in the American Negro College. Some Notes on the "Good African"*, Philon, 1970.

————, *The Kenya Masai and the Protest Phenomenon 1900 - 1960*, Journal of African History, 1971.

————, *A Biography of Molonket Olokorinya Ole Sempele*, in: K. KING - A. SALIM (eds.), Nairobi, 1971, a.

———— - SALIM, A. (eds.), *Kenya Historical Biographies*, Nairobi, 1971.

KIPURY, N. *Oral Literature of the Maasai*, Nairobi, 1983.

KITUYI, M. *Becoming Kenyans. Socio-Economic Transformation of the Pastoral Maasai*, Nairobi, 1990.

KONCZACKI, Z.A. *The Economics of Pastoralism. A Case Study of Sub-Saharan Africa*, London, 1978.

KOOIMAN, D. *Change of Religion as a Way to Survival. Some Source Material from 19th-Century Travancore*, India, in: P. QUARLES VAN UFFORD - M. SCHOFFELEERS (eds.), Amsterdam, 1988.

KWAME GYEKYE, *An Essay on African Philosophical Thought. The Akan Conceptual Scheme*, Cambridge, 1987.

LEFEBURE, C. *The Specificity of Nomadic Pastoral Societies*, in: C. LEFEBURE (ed.), Cambridge - Paris, 1979.

—————, (ed.), *Pastoral Production and Society*, Cambridge - Paris, 1979.

LEGESSE, A. *Gada. Three Approaches to the Study of African Society*, New York - London, 1973.

LE ROY, A. *Au Kilima-Ndjaro*, Bruxelles, 1894.

LEVINE, R.A. - CAMPBELL, D.T. *Ethnocentrism: Theories of Conflict, Ethnic Attitudes and Group Behavior*, New York - London, 1972.

LEWIS, I.M. *A Pastoral Democracy*, London, 1961.

LEWIS, O. *Life in a Mexican Village. Tepoztlán Restudied*, Urbana, 1951.

LEYS, N. *Kenya*, London, 1924.

MAINGA, M. *A History of Lozi Religion to the End of the Nineteenth Century*, in: T.O. RANGER - I. KIMAMBO (eds.), London, 1972.

MARX, E. *The Ecology and Politics of Nomadic Pastoralists in the Middle East*, in: W. WEISSLEIDER (ed.), Den Haag - Paris, 1978.

MATSON, A.T. *Nandi Resistance to British Rule*, Nairobi, 1972.

MAURIER, H. *Religions africaines: les pasteurs*, Vivant Univers, no. 356, 1985.

MBITI, J. *African Religions and Philosophy*, London, 1969.

—————, *New Testament Eschatology in an African Background*, London, 1971.

MEISTER, A. *L'Afrique peut-elle partir? Changement social et développement en Afrique Orientale*, Paris, 1966.

MERRILL, R.S. *Resistance to Economic Change*, Proceedings of the Minnesota Academy of Science, 1960.

MOL, F. *Maa. A Dictionary of the Maasai Language and Folklore*, Nairobi, 1978.

MONOD, T. *Introduction*, in: T. MONOD (ed.), London, 1975.

————, (ed.), *Pastoralism in Tropical Africa*, London, 1975.

MUNGEAM, G.H. *British Rule in Kenya, 1895-1912: The Establishment of Administration in the East Africa Protectorate*, Oxford, 1966.

————, *Masai and Kikuyu Responses to the Establishment of Administration in the East Africa Protectorate*, Journal of African History, 1970.

MUNRO, J.F. *Colonial Rule and the Kamba. Social Change in the Kenya Highlands 1889-1939*, Oxford, 1975.

MUTISO, G.C. *Kitui Ecosystem, Integration and Change*, in: B.A. OGOT (ed.), Nairobi, 1979.

MWAURA, P. *The Battle of Armageddon*, Inside Kenya Today, 1971.

NECKEBROUCK, V. *L'Afrique Noire et la crise religieuse de l'Occident*, Tabora, 1971.

————, *Le onzième commandement. Etiologie d'une Eglise indépendante au pied du mont Kenya*, Immensee, 1978.

————, *Le peuple affligé. Les déterminants de la fissiparité dans un nouveau mouvement religieux au Kenya Central*, Immensee, 1983.

OGOT, B.A. (ed.), *Ecology and History in East Africa*, Nairobi, 1979.

O'LEARY, M. *The Kitui Akamba. Economic and Social Change in Semi-Arid Kenya*, Nairobi, 1984.

OLE KULET, H. *Is it Possible?*, Nairobi, 1971.

————, *To Become a Man*, Nairobi, 1972.

OLE MPAAYEI, J.T. *Inkuti Pukunot ool Maasai*, Oxford, 1954.

OLE SAIBULL, S. - CARR, R. *Herd and Spear. The Maasai of East Africa*, London, 1981.

OLE SAITOTI, T. *Maasai*, London, 1980.

————, *The Worlds of a Maasai Warrior. An Autobiography*, Berkeley - Los Angeles, 1988.

ORR, J.B. - GILKS. F.R. *The Physique and Health of Two African Tribes*, London, 1931.

PHILIP, A. *New Day in Kenya*, London - New York, 1936.

PRIEST, D. *Doing Theology with the Maasai*, Pasadena, 1990.

QUARLES VAN UFFORD, P. - SCHOFFELEERS, M. (eds.), *Religion and Development. Towards an Integrated Approach*, Amsterdam, 1988.

RANGER, T.O. *The Role of Ndebele and Shona Religious Authorities in the Rebellions of 1896 and 1897*, in: E. STOKES - R. BROWN (eds.), Manchester, 1966.

————, *The Churches, the Nationalist State and African Religion*, in: E. FASHOLE-LUKE (ed.), London, 1978.

———— - KIMAMBO, I. (eds.), *The Historical Study of African religion*, London, 1972.

REDFIELD, R. *Tepoztlán, A Mexican Village. A Study of Folk Life*, Chicago, 1930.

RICOEUR, P. (ed.), *Les cultures et le temps*, Paris, 1975.

RIGBY, P. *Les retombées théoriques des stratégies de développement pastoral en Afrique Orientale*, in: J. GALATY - D. ARONSON - P.C. SALZMAN (eds.), Ottawa, 1983.

————, *Persistent Pastoralists. Nomadic Societies in Transition*, London, 1985.

ROBERTS, J. *A Land Full of People. Kenya Today*, London, 1967.

ROTBERG, R.I. (ed.), *Colonialism and Hunger: East and Central Africa*, Massachusetts - Toronto, 1983.

ROUMEGUERE-EBERHARDT, J. *Les Maasai, guerriers de la savane*, Paris, 1984.

SAHLINS, M. *Culture and Practical Reason*, Chicago, 1976.

SALZMAN, P.C. *Ideology and Change in Middle Eastern Tribal Societies*, Man, 1978.

————, *Inequality and Oppression in Nomadic Society*, in: C. LEFEBURE, (ed.), Cambridge - Paris, 1979.

————, (ed.), *When Nomads Settle. Processes of Sedenta-rization as Adaptation and Response*, New York, 1980.

SANDFORD, G.R. *An Administrative and Political History of the Masai Reserve*, London, 1919.

SCHNEIDER, H.K. *Pokot Resistance to Change*, in: W.R. BASCOM - M.J. HERSKOVITS (eds.), Chicago, 1959.

————, *Livestock and Equality in East Africa: The Economic Basis for Social Structure*, Bloomington, 1979.

SEGAL, R.A. *In Defense of Reductionism*, Journal of the American Academy of Religion, 1983.

—————, *Response to Blasi and Nelson*, Journal for the Scientific Study of Religion, 1986.

—————, *Religionist and Social Scientific Strategies*, Religion, 1989.

—————, *Religion and the Social Sciences. Essays on the Confrontation*, Atlanta, 1989.

SHINGLEDECKER, K. *Unreached Peoples Project. Maasai Report*, Nairobi, 1982.

—————, *Unreached Peoples of Kenya. A Summary Report of Research*, Nairobi, 1984.

SPENCER, I.R. *Pastoralism and Colonial Policy in Kenya, 1895-1929*, in: R.I. ROTBERG (ed.), Massachusetts - Toronto, 1983.

SPENCER, P. *The Samburu. A Study of Gerontocracy in a Nomadic Tribe*, London, 1965.

—————, *The Maasai of Matapato. A Study of Rituals of Rebellion*, Manchester - London, 1988.

STAFFNER, H. *The Significance of Jesus Christ in Asia*, Anand, 1985.

STOKES, E. - BROWN, R. (eds.), *The Zambezian Past*, Manchester, 1966.

SUTTER, J.W. *Cattle and Inequality: Herd Size Differences and Pastoral production among the Fulani of Northeastern Senegal*, Africa. Journal of the International African Institute, 1987.

TALAL ASSAD, *Equality in Nomadic Social Systems? Notes towards the Dissolution of an Anthropological Category*, in: C. LEFEBURE (ed.), Cambridge - Paris, 1979.

TALLE, A. *Women at a Loss. Changes in Maasai Pastoralism and their Effects on Gender Relations*, Stockholm, 1988.

THOMSON, J. *Through Masai Land. A Journey of Exploration among Snowclad Volcanic Mountains and Strange Tribes of Eastern Equatorial Africa*, London, 1885.

TIGNOR, R.L. *The Maasai Warriors: Pattern Maintenance and Violence in Colonial Kenya*, Journal of African History, 1972.

—————, *The Colonial Transformation of Kenya. The Kamba, Kikuyu and Maasai from 1900 to 1939*, Princeton, 1976.

84

TURNER, V. *The Ritual process. Structure and Anti-Structure*, Harmondsworth, 1974.

VAN ZWANENBERG, R. - KING, K. *An Economic History of Kenya and Uganda 1800 - 1970*, Nairobi, 1975.

VAUGHAN, J.H. *A Reconsideration of Divine Kingship*, in: I. KARP - C.S. BIRD (eds.), Bloomington, 1980.

VOSHAAR, J. *Tracing God's Walking Stick in Maa*, Licence Thesis, Catholic University of Nijmegen, 1979.

WAGNER, C.P. - DAYTON, E.R. *Unreached Peoples*, Elgin, 1978.

WALLER, R.D. *The Lords of East Africa: The Maasai in the Mid-Nineteenth Century (1840-1885)*, Ph.D. Dissertation, University of Cambridge, 1978.

——————, *Economic and Social Relations in the Central Rift Valley: The Maa-Speakers and Their Neighbors in the Nineteenth Century*, Unpublished Paper, cited in J. ILIFFE, Cambridge, 1987.

WEISSLEIDER, W. (ed.), *The Nomadic Alternative. Modes and Models of Interaction in the African-Asian Deserts and Steppes*, Den Haag - Paris, 1978.

WINKELMAN, M. *Magico-Religious Practitioner Types and Socio-Economic Conditions*, Behavioral Science Research, 1986.

WRIGHT, R. (ed.), *African Philosophy: An Introduction*, Washington, 1977.

WYLLIE, R.W. *On the Rationality of the Devout Opposition*, Journal of Religion in Africa, 1980.

ZAHAN, D. *Religion, spiritualité et pensée africaines*, Paris, 1970.

Finito di stampare il 14 maggio 1993
Tipografia Poliglotta della Pontificia Università Gregoriana
Piazza della Pilotta, 4 – 00187 Roma